SAINT
VINCENT FERRER

O.P.

BY

FR. STANISLAUS M. HOGAN, O.P.

Nihil obstat:

    R.P.F. AMBROSIUS COLEMAN, O.P., S.T.L.

    R.P.F. AUGUSTINUS DALTON, O.P., B.A., S.T.L.

Imprimatur:

    A.R.P. F. MICHAEL O'KANE, O.P., S.T.L.
    Prior Prov. Hiberniæ.

Censor Deputatus:

    R.P. J. N. STRASSMAIER, S.J.

Imprimatur:

    A.R. EDMUNDUS CANONICUS SURMONT.
    Vic. Gen. Westmonasteriensis.

PREFATORY NOTICE.

FOUR volumes of the "Friar Saints" Series are now published, and two more will be issued shortly, one Dominican dealing with "St. Pius V.," by C. M. Antony; and one Franciscan dealing with "St. John Capistran," by Fr. Vincent Fitzgerald, O.F.M.

The Series, which has received the warm approval of the authorities of both Orders in England, Ireland, and America, is earnestly recommended to Tertiaries, and to the Catholic public generally.

The Master-General of the Dominicans at Rome, sending his blessing to the writers and readers of the "Friar Saints" Series, says: "The Lives should teach their readers not only to know the Saints, but also to imitate them".

The Minister-General of the Franciscans, Fr. Denis Schuler, sends his blessing and best wishes for the success of the "Lives of the Friar Saints".

> FR. OSMUND, O.F.M., PROVINCIAL,
> FR. BEDE JARRETT, O.P.,
> C. M. ANTONY,
> *Editors.*

AMICO

V. McN.

AMICUS

D.

PREFACE.

THIS life of one of the greatest of the "Friar Saints" is based on the "Histoire de Saint Vincent Ferrier," by Père Fages, O.P. As the "Histoire" is the best and most critical life of the Saint which has been published, we have accepted the conclusions, dates, etc., of the learned author in preference to those of the Bollandists. We have tried to put the missionary journeys of St. Vincent as prominently as possible before our readers, and this will explain two or three chapters which may seem to be somewhat dry reading. But we have not given a detailed history of these journeys by any means, for the simple reason that such an account of the travels of this extraordinary man who, in his zeal for souls, traversed the length and breadth of Europe, and visited almost every city, town and village of importance in Spain, France, and Northern

Italy, would have been impossible in the short space at our disposal. We sincerely hope that this short sketch will help to stir up devotion to the Saint who preached " the unsearchable riches of Christ" in an age that was as blind and indifferent to " the things that are of the Spirit of God " as is our own.

The illustrations are reproduced from the volumes by Père Fages, O.P., so often quoted in these pages. We offer him publicly our thanks for his kindness to us in this as in other ways.

CONTENTS.

THE Holy Father has expressed his great pleasure and satisfaction that the " Friar Saints " Series has been undertaken ; and wishes it every success. He bestows " most affectionately " His Apostolic Blessing upon the Editors, Writers, and Readers of the whole Series.

CHAPTER I.

BIRTH, EARLY YEARS, FRIAR-PREACHER.

ST. VINCENT FERRER, the second son and fourth of the eight children with which the union of William Ferrer and Constance Miguel was blessed, was born at Valencia in Spain on 23 January, 1350.[1]

The house in which he was born may still be seen in the *Calle del Mar:* the room is now an oratory with the miraculous fountain and the statue of St. Vincent carved out of the cypress-tree as he foretold it should be.[2]

The Ferrers were of English origin. Amongst those who took part in the conquest of Valencia in 1238 were Bernard Ferrer, fourth son of William de Ferrariis, Earl of Derby, and Ansias Ferrer, a

[1] Fages, " Histoire de Saint Vincent Ferrier," Vol. I, p. 14; " Notes et Documents," pp. 17-24. The date of the Saint's birth is disputed. Razzano, his earliest biographer, gives the year 1346; the Bollandists give 1357. Père Fages, however, has given strong proofs in favour of the year 1350 as the correct date of St. Vincent's birth.

[2] Cf. " Histoire," p. 30; " Notes et Documents," pp. 25-32.

Scottish lord. Both had been ennobled by James
I of Aragon, but only Bernard's descendants continued to rank amongst the Spanish nobility. Our
Saint, therefore, was probably descended from Ansias
Ferrer, since in all public records his family is mentioned as belonging to the *Ciudadans*, or commoners,
as distinguished from the *Caballeros*, or gentry.[1]

Before our Saint's birth his father had a dream
in which he seemed to be present at a sermon
preached by a Dominican Friar. Suddenly the
preacher interrupted his discourse to tell William
Ferrer that a son would soon be born to him who
should become a Dominican and whose fame
should spread throughout the world. Constance
experienced a wonderful gladness during her preg-
nancy instead of the pain and lassitude she usually
felt; and one day when giving alms to a blind
woman she was accustomed to help she begged
her to pray for her safe delivery. The woman was
enlightened to prophesy. "O ! happy mother,"
she exclaimed, "it is an angel that you bear, and
one day he will give me my sight."[2]

So great was the impression made by these in-
cidents that the City Council held a special meeting
at which it was decided that the magistrates should
act as sponsors. Raymund d'Oblitès, Chief Magis-

[1] "Histoire," p. 7; "Notes et Documents," pp. 4-16.
[2] Cf. "Histoire," pp. 12-13; "Acta Sanctorum," p. 483.
Other signs are mentioned by the "Acta"; the "Année
Dominicaine" (p. 152); "Three Catholic Reformers" (p. 4).

strate, William d'Espigol, and Dominic Aragones were chosen; and the godmother was Doña Raymunda d'Encarroz y Villaragut.[1]

But at the ceremony which took place on 23 January, in the Church of St. Stephen, a difficulty arose regarding the name to be given. The parish priest, Don Perot Pertusa, settled the question by calling the child after the Saint whose feast was being celebrated at the time, and for whom the Spaniards generally, and the people of Valencia in particular, had a special devotion—St. Vincent the Martyr. The name was prophetic. The new Vincent was to become in God's own time a conqueror of Kingdoms and Souls.[2]

From his cradle the hand of God rested on Vincent Ferrer, who received the gift of miracles on the same day that he received the grace of baptism. As a child of 5 years he cured the son of Michael Garrigues of a fetid ulcer in the neck; and when Vincent was canonized, the son of him he had healed placed an image of the Saint over the door of his house. If every one who had been cured by St. Vincent Ferrer had done likewise, says an old chronicler, all Europe would be filled with monuments in his honour. But of St. Vincent as a Wonder-worker we shall speak in another chapter.

---

[1] " Histoire," p. 16 ; " Notes et Documents," pp. 21-23.

[2] *Ibid.* The *Pila* or baptismal font remains in the Church of St. Stephen. Another Dominican Saint was baptized at the same font—St. Louis Bertrand.

All the Saint's biographers speak of his remarkable beauty, the faint reflection of the inward beauty
of a soul which was wholly given to God.   This
soul-beauty of grace he ever kept intact and un-
tarnished by a life of prayer and self-denial.   He
loved to assist at sermons, particularly those on Our
Blessed Lady, for whom he had a childlike love.
Each hour he saluted her by invoking her name
and claiming her protection ; each day he recited
her Office together with the Office of the Passion.[1]

Every Wednesday and Friday he kept a strict
fast.   He learned this practice from his parents and
observed it faithfully all his life.   His love of the
poor was very great, and Razzano tells us that his
parents having allowed him to use one-third of his
inheritance, Vincent distributed it amongst the poor
in four days.[2]

Gifted in an exceptional measure with a keen in-
telligence and powers of judgment, we are scarcely
surprised to learn that he soon outdistanced his
companions when he began his classical studies at
at the age of eight.   But it is something of a surprise to hear he had finished his course of philo-

[1] " Année Dominicaine," p. 154; Fages, " Histoire,"
p. 22.   Teyxidor says it was St. Vincent who began the
custom, followed by so many preachers, of reciting the *Ave
Maria* before the sermon (" Notes et Documents," p. 34).

[2] " Année Dominicaine," p. 154 ; " Acta Sanctorum, p.
484.

sophy and begun the study of theology when he
was only fourteen ! [1]

His parents beheld a brilliant future for their son
and had obtained certain benefices for him; but
Vincent heard another voice summoning him to
"leave all things," and like Francis of Assisi,
"naked to follow the naked Christ". He obeyed
the summons, and on 2 February, 1367, Vincent
Ferrer asked to be received as a member of the
Order of Preachers in the Priory of Valencia.
Three days later, on the feast of St. Agatha, he
was clothed in the Dominican habit by the Prior,
Father Matthew de Benincasa, and began his religious life under the guidance of Father Arnaud
Sacerdol, his Novice-Master. He was then in his
eighteenth year. [2]

Earnestly did he set himself to follow in the
footsteps of his Father, St. Dominic. Like him
he sealed himself with the marks of the Crucified
by a life of rigid mortification and penance. His
fervour excited the hatred of the spirits of Evil,
who subjected him to their hellish assaults in various ways and on many occasions. Satan appeared
in the guise of a venerable hermit and urged him
to spare himself and to moderate those penances
which, he declared, were more than human nature

[1] Fages, "Histoire," p. 21 ; Bayle, "Vie de S. Vincent
Ferrier," pp. 9-10.

[2] Fages, "Histoire," p. 35; cf. "Notes et Documents,"
p. 37.

could endure. Vincent had recourse to prayer, and the tempter fled.[1]

He was tempted to despair; tempted to take what joy he could from life at the sacrifice of his virginal purity; and, hardest of all perhaps, he had to resist the tears of his mother, who besought him to leave the Order and become a secular priest. But resist he did, though his heart was like lead within him. He was strengthened to fight against "flesh and blood" as he had been nerved to resist "principalities and powers," by that other " Mother of Fair Love " to whom he had recourse, and who consoled him with words that were audible even to the human ear. [2]

His period of probation at an end, Vincent Ferrer became Christ's vassal until death by pronouncing his solemn vows on the feast of St. Dorothea, 6 February, 1368.[3]

On September 8 of the same year he was sent to begin his Dominican studies at Tarragona. Two years later he was appointed Lector of Philosophy at Lerida by the Chapter held in Valencia on 11 June, 1370. He remained three years at Lerida and was then sent to the House of Studies at Barcelona on 8 September, 1373, to study Scripture

[1] "Histoire," p. 47; "Acta Sanctorum," p. 486; "Année Dominicaine," p. 156.

[2] "Histoire," pp. 38, 47; "Acta," p. 486; Bayle, op. cit., pp. 19-20.

[3] "Notes et Documents," p. 38.

and Hebrew.[1] While studying at Barcelona and only in Deacon's orders he was bidden to preach. Famine and plague were raging. The ships sent from Flanders with corn had not arrived and the people were in despair. Vincent organized a procession, and in the *Place del Boru* preached to some 20,000 persons. The spirit of prophecy came upon him and he foretold that before nightfall the overdue ships should arrive. When he returned to the Convent it was to meet with a severe reprimand from the Prior, who bade him leave aside such predictions for the future. But that night a crowd of people rushed to the Convent, exultant, delirious with joy: the corn-laden ships had arrived and Vincent's prophecy was fulfilled.[2]

Perhaps it was to test his humility, or to save him from a people's praise that he was sent to Toulouse in 1377. We do not know, though we may well believe it was so. Vincent was sent, however, and remained a year at Toulouse. Study followed prayer, prayer succeeded study, as St. Jerome tells us should be the case, and as St. Vincent himself taught us.[3]

He had already taught Philosophy as we have seen, at Lerida, and had published a volume " De

---

[1] " Histoire," p. 40; " Notes et Documents," pp. 39-40.

[2] " Histoire," p. 41; " Notes et Documents," p. 41; " Acta Sanctorum," p. 497.

[3] " Instructio Vitæ Spiritualis, Cap. IX; " Traité de la Vie Spirituelle, Edition Rousset, Chap. VIII.

Suppositionibus Dialecticis," and a treatise " De Natura Universalis " which were held in high repute at the time.[1]

Hence when he went to Toulouse it was as a mature and proficient student who was able to profit by all the advantages which the University of Toulouse, famous for its teaching, famous too since the relics of the Angel of the Schools had been confided to it, could offer him.[2]

At the end of the year Vincent returned once again to Valencia, there to meet with fresh trials and to come face to face with the tempter in human form.   Not only was he assailed by the powers of darkness, but at least two erring women sought to make shipwreck of his virtue.   He overcame these trials as he had overcome his former temptations and came   forth   from   the   conflict strong and unscathed.[3]   He had proved himself. He had been tested by temptation and had remained firm.   He was worthy, therefore, to offer sacrifice ; and when Peter de Luna came as Papal Legate to solicit the support of the King of Aragon in favour of Clement VII, he sent for Vincent Ferrer and ordained him priest at Barcelona in 1379.[4]

[1] " Notes et Documents," p. 42.

[2] Cf. " St. Thomas of Aquin and the City and University of Toulouse," by the present writer, in the " Austral Light," November, 1908.

[3] " Histoire," pp. 45-49 ; " Notes et Documents, p. 45; " Acta Sanctorum," pp. 486-88 ; Allies, op. cit., pp. 19-20.

[4] " Histoire," p. 50; " Notes et Documents," pp. 45-46.

CHAPTER II.

FIRST LABOURS IN THE VINEYARD.

TOWARDS the end of this same year, 1379, St. Vincent was elected Prior of Valencia, and on taking office he began to urge the claims of Clement VII.[1]

This occasioned some dispute between him and the Magistrates, who, following the example of the King of Aragon, refused to take sides with Clement VII, or Urban VI. Unable to win their adherence, Vincent resigned his Priorship; but a proof of the friendly relations which still existed between him and them, and of the reverence in which he was held, is to be had in the fact that the Magistrates invited the late Prior to preach the Lenten Sermons in the Cathedral in 1381.[2]

In 1345, Raymund Gaston, Bishop of Valencia,

---

[1] A letter from the Magistrates of Valencia to Peter IV, King of Aragon, speaks of St. Vincent as Prior of the Convent at Valencia. The letter is dated 14 December, 1379, and is published by Père Fages ("Notes et Documents," pp. 46-47).

[2] Fages, "Histoire," pp. 51-54; "Notes et Documents," p. 51. The Saint composed another treatise about this time, "De Schismo," which is published by Père Fages in his edition of the "Œuvres de S. Vincent Ferrier".

had established a Chair of Theology in the Cathedral
and had confided it to the Order of Preachers for
ever.[1]

These lectures were greatly esteemed, and were
attended not by priests only but by laymen, physicians and lawyers. In 1385, the Bishop and
Chapter appointed St. Vincent to give the lectures.
He gave his inaugural lecture on 9 December,
and continued the course until 1390.[2]

In 1386, we find him preaching the Lenten
Sermons at Segovia[3]; and in 1390, at the conclu-
sion of his lectures at Valencia, he received his
Doctor's degree.[4]

His name appears in various judicial documents
at this time, and a decree of the Municipal Council,

[1] Fages, " Notes et Documents," p. 55.

[2] Fages, " Histoire," p. 55. " Notes et Documents,"
pp. 56-57. The room in his brother's house where St. Vincent lodged when he gave the lectures is still to be seen
opposite the Migueléte. It is now an oratory, but thanks
to the piety and reverence of its owners, nothing has been
changed in it.

[3] In this year the Infante Don Martin founded the Carthusian Monastery of *Val Christo*, whither Boniface Ferrer
retired in 1395, becoming General of the Order some years
later. Cf. " Année Dominicaine, p. 165.

[4] Fages, " Histoire," p. 59. Some writers say the Saint
went to Paris and Rome, and that he received his degree as
Doctor Parisiensis. There is no evidence that this was the
case, just as evidence is also wanting to prove that he
received his degree at Lerida. Most probably it was con-
ferred on him by Clement VII, at the request of Peter de
Luna.

dated 15 April, 1390, orders "a hundred gold florins to be distributed to those repentant women converted by Father Vincent Ferrer, so that they may be honourably married ".[1]

In August, 1390, Peter de Luna returned to Valencia. Castile had declared in favour of Clement VII, in 1381, and Aragon had followed suit in 1387. The Legate had relied on St. Vincent for help and had not relied in vain. The Saint was respected by all; he was a marvellous preacher, a man whose convincing eloquence had converted the famous Jewish Rabbi, Paul of Burgos, who died Bishop of Carthagena in 1435. The Legate wished to bring our Saint back with him to Avignon, but Vincent had a work to do which kept him in Spain. In the uprising against the Jews of Valencia in July, 1391, he proved himself to be their friend, father, and protector, a fact which the Jews themselves recognized in a very marked manner.[2]

Some writers are only too ready to speak of *los males causados por Fray Vincente*, and represent him as a "mad fanatic" whose "brutality and cruelty should be proverbial ".[3]

History, however, that is, history which is based on facts and documents and not the romance which is misnamed history, tells us the contrary; and

[1] Fages, "Histoire, p. 63; "Notes et Documents," pp. 70-72.

[2] Cf. Fages, " Histoire," pp. 66-70.

[3] Cf. "Cities of Spain," by Edward Hutton, London, 1909, p. 181.

neither in Valencia nor Toledo did St. Vincent
Ferrer rouse "the people   to fury till they
massacred the Jews," as Mr. Hutton informs us.
It is unhappily only too true that for a certain class
of writers and of readers romance is more accept-
able than prosaic facts.[1]

At Valencia, St. Vincent went amongst the Jews,
consoling them, instructing them, exhorting them
to seek baptism.   It is very probable that many
were baptized merely to escape persecution, but the
sincerity of the Jews of Valencia and their esteem
for the man who befriended them is sufficiently established by their constancy and perseverance in
the faith.[2]   A Confraternity of Jews who had been
converted by our Saint existed for many years in
Valencia.   It was rich and generous too, and on
more than one occasion gave proof of its generosity
and gratitude by giving large donations to the religious brethren of him who had converted them.

About this time, Queen Yolande accompanied
King John I to Valencia.   But when her husband
was obliged to leave shortly after in order to defend

---

[1] Mr. Hutton grows lachrymose because the Mosque at
Toledo was "desecrated" by being turned into a church—
S. Maria la Blanca. His grief is assuaged, however, by the
fact that: "To-day   S. Maria la Blanca is in the
hands of the Government, which after so long has at last
rescued it from the Church of Spain " (" Cities of Spain,"
pp. 182-83).

[2] Teyxidor, *ap*. Fages, " Histoire," p. 69 ; " Notes et.
Documents," pp. 78-86.

Sicily and Sardinia against the Moors, the Queen remained, most probably until the birth of her son on
23 January, 1394. St. Vincent occupied the somewhat embarrassing position of Confessor to her imperious Majesty, who was most anxious to see him at
prayer in his cell, for was it not openly stated that
he prayed in ecstasy and surrounded by a heavenly
radiance? St. Vincent forbade the Queen to visit
his cell. Yolande was not to be denied, and went;
but although the Saint was visible to those who accompanied the Queen, he remained unseen by her.
"Father, where are you?" exclaimed Yolande.
"I am here," replied St. Vincent, "hidden from
your eyes. Leave at once, and understand that
God would punish you severely but that you act
through feminine curiosity."[1] When the Court left
Valencia, St. Vincent accompanied the Queen, who
revered him as a Saint and always spoke to him on
her knees; but he accompanied the Court only on
the express condition that he should be quite free
to devote himself to the work of preaching. His
fame grew apace; even the very pieces which the
people in their enthusiasm cut from his habit
wrought miracles; yet trials were not wanting. He
was accused of preaching heretical doctrines and was
summoned to appear before the Inquisition to clear
himself of the charge. Clement VII, however, had

[1] Fages, " Histoire," p. 72; Bayle, op. cit., p. 53; " Année
Dominicaine," p. 163; Allies, op. cit., p. 15; " Acta Sanctorum," p. 495.

died, and had been succeeded by Peter de Luna as
Benedict XIII.   He knew the Saint too well to
permit what Raynaldus calls a "barefaced calumny"
to continue, and so he put a stop to the proceedings,
and called St. Vincent to Avignon in 1395.[1]   The
hour was at hand when St. Vincent Ferrer was to
begin his wonderful apostolate throughout Europe.

Before we proceed farther it will be advisable to
give a brief sketch of what has been termed "The
Great Schism" in the Church, when there was a
Sovereign Pontiff at Rome and a usurper at
Avignon.   It was a time of grave trial and the
situation was unparalleled in the history of the
Church ; yet there were Saints on each side.   If
we have St. Catherine of Siena and St. Catherine of
Sweden fighting the cause of Urban VI, we have
St. Vincent Ferrer and Blessed Peter of Luxem-
bourg amongst the staunch adherents of Clement
VII and Benedict XIII.   This fact, which is suf-
ficient to show how embarrassing was the situation,
ought to prevent all hasty judgment.

The actual Schism began at the death of
Gregory XI in 1378, but events had prepared the
way for it long before that time ; amongst the circumstances which led to the Schism was the trans-
ference of the Papal Throne to Avignon, in 1309,
by Clement V.   When Gregory XI died at Rome
the College of Cardinals numbered twenty-three,

[1] Fages, "Histoire," pp. 93, 94 ; "Notes et Documents,"
pp. 90-96 ; "Année Dominicaine," p. 164 ; Bayle, op. cit.,
p. 59.

but sixteen only took part in the election, and one
of the number was Peter de Luna. Bartolomeo
Prignano, Archbishop of Bari, was elected on 8 April,
1378, and took the name of Urban VI. Mis-
understanding the impatience of the people who
loudly clamoured for an Italian Pope, and who
broke into the conclave when Urban was elected,
the Cardinals fled without having made their sub-
mission to the new Pontiff. Urban was an austere
man ; hasty and imperious, and he alienated the
sympathies of the Cardinals by speaking of reform
shortly after his election. They began to murmur
and to say the election was invalid because they
had been terrorized. Joanna of Naples fostered
the discontent and received the Cardinals at Fondi,
where they elected Cardinal Robert of Geneva as
Clement VII on 20 September of the same year.
The other Cardinals who had taken no part in the
election of Urban VI joined hands with those who
elected Clement VII. Urban created twenty-nine
new Cardinals at once, and the Schism had begun.[1]

Who was the lawful Pope? As Pastor says :
" It cannot be denied that the election of Urban
VI was canonically valid," but it " had been
brought about only by the dissensions between
the different parties and was agreeable to none ". [2]
It is comparatively easy to judge the question
impartially and dispassionately now; it was diffi-

[1] Fages, " Histoire," pp. 84-85 ; Pastor, " History of the
Popes," Vol. I, p. 117 *seqq* ; Bayle, op. cit., p. 45.
[2] Op. cit., p. 120.

cult to discriminate then between the rival claimants. We should bear in mind the circumstances
of the election and of the time in which it took
place. We should also remember that the Cardinals, upon whom the responsibility fell, protested
that they had been forced by fear into electing
Urban VI; that they stated emphatically that his
election was invalid; and that Clement VII was
the legitimate Pontiff. It was these reasons which
induced St. Vincent Ferrer to acknowledge Clement VII as the only lawful Pope, and it was
these reasons which he put forward and developed
in his treatise on "The Schism". It would be very
wrong to doubt his good faith or his conviction.[1]
Hence when Clement VII died, and Don Pedro
Martinez de Luna succeeded him as Benedict XIII,
St. Vincent acknowledged him as the lawful Pope.
It was a natural and logical proceeding. The
Schism grew more pronounced; and if it was in
reality a conflict between two nations for the possession of the Papacy[2] it cannot be denied that
the breach was widened by the obstinacy of Peter
de Luna. Loyal as St. Vincent was to Benedict
XIII, he withdrew his support when he saw that
Benedict was an obstacle to the union and peace
of the Church; and we shall see that it was in large
measure owing to the Saint that the Schism was ended
and union was restored a few years before his death.

[1] Cf. Fages, " Histoire," p. 92.
[2] Pastor, op. cit., p. 146 and note.

CHAPTER III.

AVIGNON.

AVIGNON, once the city of the Popes, is pregnant with Dominican memories. St. Dominic assisted at a Council against the Albigenses and established one of his first houses there. Two Popes lodged in this Convent while the Palace was being built. Two Conclaves were held and two Popes crowned within its walls. St. Thomas of Aquin was canonized in the Divinity School of the Convent, and a few streets are still named after the great Dominican Saints. The Convent has gone. Its very ruins have disappeared. But the Palace of the Popes dominates the city and seems to absorb it within itself.

When Peter de Luna was elected in succession to Clement VII his first care was to summon prudent and learned men to his assistance. Boniface Ferrer and Francis d'Aranda had to leave their Carthusian solitude at his command. St. Vincent Ferrer, as we have said, was also called to Avignon, and arrived about the end of 1395. Benedict XIII appointed him his Confessor and Chaplain, Apostolic Penitentiary, and Master of the Sacred Palace.[1]

[1] Fages, " Histoire," p. 105. Some doubt exists regarding this last appointment, but a volume of St. Thomas which

His position was one of extreme difficulty and delicacy, but his modesty, gentleness and firmness won him the respect and veneration of the whole Court and the friendship of Benedict XIII, though Vincent never lost his fearlessness or forfeited his religious independence.   He refused several Bishoprics, that of Valencia amongst them; and when Benedict thought to take him by surprise and make him a Cardinal, the humble friar smilingly but very decidedly refused to accept the dignity.[1] Benedict was a kindly man, a brilliant speaker, a diplomat; but excessively obstinate.   France had declared in his favour, yet tried hard to make him come to some understanding with the Pontiff at Rome.   All was in vain, however, and Benedict XIII would not move a finger to put an end to the scandal which existed.   He absolutely refused to accept the decision of the council of theologians which was held at Paris in July, 1398, when a practically unanimous judgment was given against him.[2]   On 1 September the Decree ordering the withdrawal of the obedience of the French to Benedict was solemnly published at Avignon. The city was besieged; but Benedict shut himself

belonged to Boniface Ferrer has St. Vincent's name in it with the title: " Magister Sacri Palatii"; cf. " Notes et Documents," p. 92.

[1] Fages, " Histoire," pp. 106-7; " Année Dominicaine," p. 171; Bayle, op. cit., p. 65; " Acta Sanctorum," p. 490.

[2] Fages, " Histoire," p. 109.

up in the Palace, determined to resist to the last.[1]

We can appreciate the difficulties which St. Vincent Ferrer had to face as confessor and counsellor to a man who was actually sacrificing the peace of the Church in an effort to uphold his own personal dignity. The burden grew too heavy, the anxiety too great for the Saint, who fell so seriously ill that all hopes of recovery were lost. God's hour had struck.

"Nearly fifteen years ago," St. Vincent writes to Benedict XIII in 1412, "a religious who was dangerously ill asked God to restore him to health so that he might preach His word. And as he prayed, St. Dominic and St. Francis appeared to him, kneeling and praying with him. At their prayer Our Blessed Lord appeared to the sick religious, and touching him familiarly with His All Holy Hand, made known to him in an interior manner, but very clearly, that it was his mission to go forth and preach to men even as the two Saints present had done. At the touch of that Divine Hand the religious rose up healed of his sickness. God has deigned to confirm the mission which He confided to this religious and which he has striven with his whole heart to accomplish."[2]

[1] Fages, "Histoire," p. 110; "Notes et Documents," p. 93.

[2] Fages, "Histoire," p. 113; "Notes et Documents," p. 92; Allies, op. cit., pp. 25-26; Bayle, op. cit., p. 62; "Année Dominicaine," p. 170; "Acta Sanctorum," p. 489.

The religious was St. Vincent himself, and the miracle occurred on 3 October, 1398. On that day the Saint became what he ever afterwards loved to style himself—Legate *a latere Christi.* The actual, definite vocation of the Saint to his extraordinary apostolate begins from the date of his restoration to health and his vision; and so firmly convinced was he of this Divine summons that he immediately besought Benedict XIII to allow him to begin his mission at once. Benedict refused, however, for he needed the presence and disinterested advice of the Saint too greatly to yield without a protest. At last he gave his consent; and, armed with the fullest power and authority which the Church could bestow, St. Vincent Ferrer began his Apostolate as the Legate of Jesus Christ on 22 November, 1399. During a period of twenty years he was to preach to the nations and sound the trumpet call to rise from the grave of sin and do penance. "Every step he took," says an old chronicler, "during the remaining years of his life was a miracle; every word he spoke was a conquest over sin." [1]

Contemporary evidence pictures St. Vincent at this time as a man of medium height, with a lofty forehead and very beautiful features which inspired reverence in all who beheld him. His fair hair, shaven in the form of the monastic tonsure, seemed as it were an aureola of glory around his head.

---

[1] Fages, " Histoire," p. 117; " Notes et Documents," p. 97.

His eyes were dark, large, very expressive, and full of fire which, however, was tempered by his habitually gentle manner. Pale as his ordinary colour was, he became slightly ruddy when preaching; and although this beauty faded in later years, as the result of his labours and the austerities he practised, it became changed rather than vanished, and took on a transparent glow which seemed to be the reflection of the inward beauty of his soul which was aflame with love of God and of his fellow man. His voice was strong and powerful, ringing at one time like a silver bell, again sounding like a full-toned trumpet; sweet, resonant, vibrant, it seemed to search the very heart and to inspire fear when fear was needed, or to sooth with exquisite tenderness.[1]

When St. Vincent began his Apostolate large numbers of men and women and even children attached themselves to him and followed him from place to place. The numbers varied. At one time his followers were as many as 10,000, composed of all classes, clerics and laymen, rich and poor, University professors and students, many of whom gave up all chances of worldly prosperity to accompany " Master Vincent ". By degrees, however, the numbers grew less. There was a process of "weeding," for it was only on certain conditions that any one was received into the company. Those who desired to join the Penitents of Master

[1] Cf. " Histoire," Vol. II, p. 449; Allies, op. cit., p. 13.

Vincent must have no ties, no debts, and any who were necessary for the support of their parents were absolutely refused. Married persons were received on the express condition that husband and wife should live apart; while a universal condition binding upon all was the distribution of any wealth they might possess amongst the poor. The strictest supervision was exercised; and during the processions which took place each evening the men and women walked in separate companies. During these processions the Penitents recited the Psalms and took the discipline, an act of public penance which softened more than one hard heart and made more than one proud sinner join their ranks. These followers 'of our Saint instructed the ignorant and the children, attended the sick and assisted the dying; while not infrequently did St. Vincent leave a few of these tried and trusty souls in the various cities and towns he visited, that they might continue the good work which he had begun. What is more, the men of the company gave their services in building monasteries, hospitals, churches, and we shall see that the Chapel of Folgoet at Quimper, a very gem of Gothic architecture, was built by the unnamed and unknown builders who were amongst St. Vincent's followers.[1] This company, composed as it was of all classes and of various nationalities, followed the Saint through

[1] Cf. "Histoire," Vol. I, pp. 150-58, 242; "Acta Sanctorum," pp. 491-92.

Europe, yet never once was there a breath of scandal, a circumstance well worthy of remark in an age of licence, a circumstance to which St. Vincent himself drew attention in one of his sermons.

Several priests accompanied our Saint, secular priests as well as members of various religious Orders, and some Dominicans whose names are known to us. These were Peter de Moya and John d'Alcoy who have been declared Venerable; Peter Querault, of the Counts of Querault in Catalonia, whose incorrupt body was seen as late as 1808 by Vidal y Mico; Geoffroy or Jofre de Blanès; Peter Cerdan, John de Gentilpré, Raphael de Cardorna, and Peter Colomer. Another companion whom St. Vincent loved dearly was Father Gilabert of the Order of Mercy; while at least one Carthusian, Father John Placentis, obtained permission to leave the solitude of his Carthusian cell and follow the Saint for many years. We owe Father John a deep debt of gratitudé for having preserved to us many of St. Vincent's sermons which he took down as he heard them preached fifty years later this same Carthusian gave evidence before the Commissaries at Nantes regarding the virtues and sanctity of St. Vincent whom he had served so faithfully and so well.[1]

It was the duty of these priests to assist in hearing the confessions of those who were brought

[1] "Histoire," *ibid.*, p. 144; "Notes et Documents," pp. 371-77.

back from their sinful ways by the preaching of the Saint. They also formed a choir which sang the Proper of the Mass, for the Saint sang Mass morning after morning, and had a portable organ carried on all his journeys. To these must be added a few Notaries-Public who drew up the various deeds of agreement between the enemies who were reconciled by St. Vincent.[1]

Such was the Saint : such was his company. In the fulness of power, and on fire with zeal for the souls of men, he began his work, a work that was only to cease when the toiler could labour no more.

Let us see with what success he laboured.

[1] "Acta Sanctorum," pp. 491-92.

CHAPTER IV.

THE APOSTOLATE, 1400-1406.

WHEN St. Vincent left Avignon he took the road to Carpentras where he preached in the Dominican Church in presence of the Bishop, magistrates, and an immense congregation on 24 December, 1399. From Carpentras he went to Arles, arriving there on 10 February, 1400, and in the public square which was named after him, but is now the *Place Balechou*, there yet stands the cross which was erected by the people at the time in memory of the mission.[1] He visited Sisteron for the first time in May; in August we find him preaching there again, and he paid a third and fourth visit to the place which possessed a Convent of the order, on 7 December, 1401, and 16 June, 1402.[2] From 27 October, 1400, until 1 December, he stayed at Aix, visiting Marseilles and preaching in the country around Aix. From 1401 to 1403 he was engaged in giving missions throughout Dau-

[1] Fages, " Histoire," p. 124; "Notes et Documents," p. 100. The Augustinian nuns who had charge of the hospital at Arles possess—or possessed in 1901—the pulpit from which the Saint preached.

[2] *Ibid.*, " Notes et Documents," p. 104.

phiné, Savoy and the Alpine Valleys. A letter
written by him on 17 November, 1403, to the
General of the Order, Jean de Puynoix, which is
still extant, gives us an account of his journeys.
Lucerne, Lausanne, the Valleys of Argentière and
Vanpute, and the dioceses of Sion, Tarantaise,
Grenoble, and Turin were the scenes of his labours.
Vanpute, so called because it received the rains
and waters caused by the melting snows on the
mountains (and also because it was a sink of ini-
quity), became *Valpure* when St. Vincent had
preached to its inhabitants. This name it preserved until Louis XI altered it into that of Vallouise; and Père Rossignol de Vallouise, S.J.
writing in the eighteenth century, bears witness to
the effects of the Saint's preaching which had lasted
even down to his time.[1] In his letter mentioned
above the Saint attributes the wickedness of the
people and the spread of heresy to the absence of
preachers who would break the bread of God's word
to them.[2] He did not spare himself, and his journeys
were veritable triumphal marches, "every step a
miracle ". The records which have not been lost or
destroyed speak in glowing terms of the conversions
which followed his preaching and of the countless
miracles which confirmed it. He paid several visits
to the Grande Chartreuse where Boniface was now

[1] Fages, " Histoire," p. 132; " Notes et Documents," 110-
12.

[2] *Ibid.*, pp. 129-31; " Notes et Documents," pp. 109-10.

General of the Order, and the Annals tell us that :
" God worked wonders by means of these two
brothers.   Those who were converted by the
preaching of one brother received the religious habit
from the hands of the other." [1]

But St. Vincent did not move sinners only to
repentance ; he pointed out and trained Saints.
Preaching at Alexandria he bade his hearers thank
God since one amongst them should become a
disciple of St. Francis of Assisi, the Apostle of
Italy, and though younger than himself should
nevertheless be canonized before him.   St. Vincent
was canonized in 1455 ; Bernardine of Siena, the
youth of the prophecy, was canonized in 1450. [2]
Another saintly soul who was guided by St. Vincent along the way of perfection at this time was
Blessed Margaret of Savoy.   Married to Theodore Paleologus II, and left a widow while quite
young, Margaret entered the Third Order of St.
Dominic and established a Convent in her country
residence at Alba Pompeïa, where she died on
21 November, 1464. [3]

[1] Annales Cartusiæ Ann., 1403 ; *ap.* Fages, " Notes et
Documents," p. 113.

[2] Fages, " Histoire," p. 134 ; " Année Dominicaine," pp.
185-86.   Abbé Bayle says the prophecy was uttered at
Monza, but the " Annales Fratrum Minorum " mention it
as having occurred at Alexandria (" Notes et Documents,"
p. 113).

[3] *Ibid.*, pp. 137-38 ; " Notes et Documents," pp. 116-17.
After four centuries of existence the nuns have been expelled

Of St. Vincent's labours in Piedmont we have records of the numberless conversions and of his miracles.   In fact the miraculous marks every step of the Saint's Apostolate in Italy; while scattered throughout the country are numerous wayside shrines dedicated to *San Vincenzo,* tokens of a people's gratitude to, and love of the Spanish Friar.[1]

Savoy, Switzerland, and Lyons were evangelized by him during 1403.   The people received him with enthusiasm wherever he appeared; and it is worthy of notice that he laid great stress on the efficacy of Holy Water.   He taught the people of Montecalieri to use it when hail and storms threatened to destroy their vineyards,[2] just as in later years he instructed the inhabitants of Chinchilla in Spain to use Holy Water as a remedy against locusts and other pests, sprinkling the ground and houses with it while invoking the Holy Name of Jesus.[3]   In 1405 we find him at Genoa where Marshal Boucicaut was Governor for France. This man regarded Vincent as a Saint, and we shall see later the testimony he bore to the holiness and austerity of St. Vincent's life.   But then it was only natural to revere the Apostle as a Saint, and so cer-

from their Convent by the present Italian Government, whose King belongs to the House of Savoy.   The Convent is now the village school.

[1] Fages, " Histoire," p. 143.
[2] *Ibid.,* p. 142.   [3] *Ibid.,* p. 293.

tain did his future canonization appear, that regular processes were instituted in some places even during his lifetime.[1]

Now St. Vincent himself tells us that he preached in his mother-tongue—Limousin, and that he knew "some Latin and a little Hebrew," yet all his hearers, and they included Germans, Greeks, Sardinians, Italians, and English, understood him perfectly. This gift of tongues is a thoroughly attested fact, and we possess the letter of Nicolas Clemangis, a man of probity of life as well as of undoubted learning, in testimony of the impression which this continual miracle made upon him.[2] Not only this, but his voice, rich, full, and powerful, capable of giving expression to every shade and meaning, was heard at long distances from the place where he actually preached. Gifted as he was in a remarkable degree with all the qualities which make an orator, it is hardly possible to account for or explain this phenomenon by purely natural reasons.[3]

Journeying westward, St. Vincent preached along the Riviera at Savona, Ventimiglia, and San Remo. At Savona, as in Genoa, he succeeded in persuading the ladies to change their strange style of coiffure, a circumstance which Tacchetti says, somewhat cruelly,

[1] Fages, " Histoire," p. 142; " Notes et Documents," p. 117.

[2] Fages, " Histoire," pp. 162-64 ; " Notes et Documents," p. 132.

[3] Fages " Histoire," loc. cit.

was "the greatest of all his marvellous deeds!"[1]
Embarking at some port in the south, St. Vincent
went to Flanders, where his miracles were of such
frequent occurrence that an hour was set aside each
day for the healing of the sick.[2] Brussels and
Arras were visited, and Henry IV of England invited him to preach in Great Britain. According
to Père Trouville, O.P., St. Vincent accepted the
invitation and preached in England, Scotland, and
Ireland; while an ancient tradition has it that he
visited Tallaght, near Dublin, where the Novitiate
of the Irish Dominicans is now established.[3] We
should be glad if the tradition was supported by
any solid evidence, but unfortunately as Père
Fages tells us, there are absolutely no records of
any kind in proof that the Saint ever preached in
Great Britain or Ireland. The hermitage near
Bristol which bears the name of St. Vincent's Rock,
is called after St. Vincent the Martyr.[4] The most
probable explanation is that Henry IV, who had
possessions in Flanders, invited St. Vincent to
preach throughout his dominions in that country;
but as we have said, there is no proof, no record
that the Saint ever crossed the Channel to preach
in England.

[1] Fages, "Histoire," p. 170.
[2] Choquet, "Externi SS. Dominicani qui in Belgio fuerunt"
Douai, 1627, p. 31; apud Fages, "Histoire," p. 177.
[3] Fages, "Histoire," p. 179; "Année Dominicaine," p.
184; Bayle, p. 152.
[4] "Histoire," p. 180.

It is evident that St. Vincent did not follow any definite order in his missionary journeys, but that he went to those places where the needs were greatest and as God directed him.   His steps cross and recross each other as he went up and down Europe, preaching with a zeal and fervour like to that of the Apostles themselves.   Hence we find him in Italy once more in 1406, when he preached peace and forgiveness to the Guelfs and Ghibellines who, in the persons of Facino Cane and Theodore of Montferrat, were at deadly war with each other in Vercelli.   To secure the permanence of his preaching, the Saint drew up a code of laws and statutes which received the sanction of the City Council.[1]

It is certain that the Saint preached the Lent and Advent Sermons at Clermont-Ferrand in 1407;[2] yet we also find it stated that he preached during the Lent of the same year in Genoa,[3] while Teyxidor adds to the confusion by asserting that St. Vincent came to Valencia in 1407.   The confusion arises from forgetfulness that in some countries the year began on 25 March, and ended at Easter: hence if we take 1406 as the year when the Saint preached at Vercelli; that he then went to Genoa and laboured in those provinces which

[1] Cusano, " Discours historiques sur les Evéques de Verceil," 1672; Corbellini, " Istoria dei Vescovi di Vercelli," 1674; *apud* Fages, " Histoire," p. 183 ; cf. " Notes et Documents," p. 134.

[2] Fages, " Notes et Documents," p. 137.

[3] *Ibid.*, p. 138.

acknowledged Benedict XIII, and at the end of this year 1406, i.e. at the beginning of 1407, he returned to Genoa and embarked for La Rochelle or Bordeaux, the confusion is somewhat lessened. Part of the year 1407 was occupied in missionary labours in the south-west provinces of France, and towards the end of the year the Saint preached in the Central Provinces, going as far as Lyons. He then retraced his steps, and journeying down the Rhône, set sail for Genoa a third time, making a longer stay in the vicinity than usual, since we learn that he preached at the Provincial Chapter which was held at Savona, on Low Sunday, 1408.[1]

Yet the Saint was sorely troubled, and anxiety preyed upon him to such an extent that he almost became as ill as on a previous occasion owing to the obstinacy of Benedict XIII. Every effort had been made to bring the Schism to an end, but Benedict, despite his professed desire for peace, would not yield, and Gregory XII, the Roman Pontiff, was as little disposed to abdicate as was his rival.[2] St. Vincent was unable to bear the weight and responsibility, particularly since Benedict would not pay any attention to his remonstrances, and he turned his face towards Spain and sailed for Corunna. He made the pilgrimage to the Shrine of St. James of Compostella, as he tells us in one of

---

[1] Fages, "Histoire," pp. 185-86 ; " Notes et Documents," pp. 137-39.

[2] Cf. Pastor, op. cit., p. 175.

his sermons, and laboured there and also at Oviedo.[1]
While at Compostella a blind man came from
Oviedo and asked St. Vincent to cure him. The
Saint bade him return to Oviedo and, kneeling be-
fore the Crucifix in the Cathedral, to tell our Lord
that Father Vincent had sent him to be cured.
The man obeyed, and his faith was rewarded by the
gift of sight.[2]

At the time when St. Vincent preached in Spain,
Grenada was under the Moorish yoke and Ma-
homet Aben Balva was enthroned in the Alhambra.
Hearing of St. Vincent he sent for him and begged
him to preach to his people. The Saint consented
willingly, and such was his eloquence and force of
argument that some 8000 Moors asked to be baptized. The King himself was disposed to embrace
the faith, but he was a weakling; and when the
Alfaquirs, or Moorish priests, threatened to re-
nounce their allegiance to him if he gave up his
faith in the Prophet, Aben Balva grew afraid.
Sending for St. Vincent, he thanked him for all he
had done and requested him to leave Grenada.[3]
Seville, Cordova, and Ecija were visited, and in
Seville he preached in the open, beneath the shadow
of the Giralda, since there was no church spacious

---

[1] Fages, " Histoire," pp. 186-87. " Notes et Documents,"
p. 139.

[2] *Ibid.*, " Notes et Documents," p. 140; Allies, op. cit.,
p. 44.

[3] *Ibid.*, " Histoire," p. 188; Allies, p. 58; " Acta," p.
494.

enough to accommodate those who came to his sermons.   It was the same at Cordova.   Toledo was
also visited at this time, and St. Vincent roused the
drooping spirits of the Christians, who were tyran-
nized over by both Jews and Mussulmans to such
an extent that they had lost even the desire to as-
sert their rights.   Castelar, in 1869, attacked the
memory of St. Vincent by accusing him of having
stirred up the Christian Community to massacre
the Jews.   We do not think it is necessary to reply
to such a calumny, emanating from a man who per-
secuted the Church in Spain.   It is just possible
that the Christians, goaded beyond endurance, did
retaliate.   The cruel martyrdom of the *Santo Niño
de la Guardia* by the Jews in mockery of Our Lord
is not by any means an isolated fact.   Castelar did
not refer to this fact as a possible reason for, and
explanation of, the massacre.   His sole desire was
to vilify a Saint.

Avila, Siguentes, and Madrid received the
Apostle, but when he preached at Cuenca the
abandoned women of the place attacked the house
where he lodged and drove him from the town.[1]
He preached at Burgos; and Victoria, the ecclesi-
astical capital of the Basque provinces, where his
preaching bore witness again to his gift of tongues,
still numbers several families who proudly trace
their descent from the Jews who were converted

[1] Fages, " Histoire," p. 196.

by "Master Vincent".[1]   San Sebastian, Tolosa,
and Mondragon were visited in turn by the Saint,
and then, obedient to the commands of Benedict
XIII, he set out for Perpignan, where the Pontiff
with all solemnity opened a Council on the Feast of
All Saints, 1408.

[1] Fages, " Histoire," p. 196.

CHAPTER V.

"IN JOURNEYINGS OFTEN," 1408-1412.

IT does not enter into the purpose of this volume to discuss the so-called "Council" of Perpignan except to state that St. Vincent took part in the proceedings at the direct command of Benedict XIII, and that in company with the others present he acknowledged Benedict as the lawful Pope. But it must also be stated that he urged the Pontiff to resign as the most effectual way of restoring peace and union to the Church. Benedict consented to the proposal, but failed to keep his promise, and the Schism continued. Towards the end of November St. Vincent left Perpignan, though the "Council" was not over, and arrived at Montpellier on the 29th of the month. He preached to the people in his own tongue on "Mossenhor San Andrieu," taking the words: The Lord is rich to all those that call upon Him (Rom. x. 12) for his text,[1] and visited the various convents of nuns around Montpellier itself. He proceeded to Nîmes where another incident which certainly cannot be explained by any

[1] Fages, " Histoire," pp. 203-05 ; " Notes et Documents," p. 140.

36

natural means, occurred, when a monk in the Abbey
of Villeneuve-lez-Avignon, twenty-five miles away,
heard the sermon preached by St. Vincent at
Nîmes.[1]

Returning to Perpignan, he received a letter
from Don Martin, King of Aragon, beseeching him
to come to his assistance as soon as possible, as he
wished to consult him on a matter of gravest importance.[2] St. Vincent set out immediately, preaching at Elne, Ulla and Gerone in Catalonia on his
journey. The steps of the Dominican Church at
Gerone from which the Saint preached bear an inscription to the effect that 20,000 persons were
present at his sermon, and give the verses which
the Saint told his hearers would be sung by the
angels on the Day of Judgment as they accompanied
the blessed to heaven.[3] Before leaving Gerone,
the Saint wrought a miracle which made a deep impression on those who witnessed it. A jealous and
suspicious husband had accused his wife of adultery,

---

[1] Fages, " Histoire," p. 206.

[2] The question regarded the right of succession (Fages,
" Histoire," p. 212).

[3] The inscription tells us the exact date when St. Vincent
preached: April 13th, 1409. The verses run as follows :—

> Felix dies !   Felix hora !
> Felix tempus !   Felix mora !
>   Quibus peccata demisisti !
> Felix dies ! etc.   Quibus Christo adhesisti !
> Felix dies ! etc.   Quibus penitentiam egisti !

Cf. Fages, " Notes et Documents," p. 156.

and refused to acknowledge his child which he protested was not his.   St. Vincent bade the injured
wife to bring the little one to his next sermon and to
beg her husband to come too.   During the sermon,
the Saint commanded the baby to go to its father,
and the child of eight months old, leaving its mother's
arms, stretched out its hands to the man who had
repudiated it.   The miracle changed and softened
his heart, and peace was restored.[1]

From Gerone the Saint passed through Vicq and
Granollers, arriving at Barcelona on 14 June.   The
King came to meet him ; the Bishop and Chapter,
as well as the magistrates of the city were full of
enthusiasm ; and Barcelona was in a state of excitement and fervour which lasted during the six
weeks that St. Vincent passed within its walls.
Miracles confirmed the preaching of the Apostle,
some of them of a startling character which could
not fail to produce a lasting impression ; and it was
in memory of the vision which St. Vincent had of
Barcelona's Angel Guardian, that the gate which
was called the Gate of the Blind became the Gate
of the Guardian-Angel, and had a chapel built over
it with a statue of the angelic defender of the
city.[2]

---

[1] Fages, " Histoire," p. 212 ; Bayle, op. cit., p. 166 ; cf.
Fages, " Notes et Documents," p. 157.

[2] *Ibid.*, pp. 221-22 ; the gate opened on the famous
Rambla, " the one beautiful street in the city," as Mr.
Hutton styles it. Both chapel and gate have been destroyed,

The King of Aragon as we have seen had written to the Saint begging him to come to his assistance in a matter of grave importance. Martin the Elder, as he was called, was the second son of Pedro IV, and had ascended the throne in 1355, as King of Aragon and Sicily. He gave the government of Sicily to his son, Martin the Younger, who when Sardinia, which was held in fief of Aragon, rose in revolt, defeated the revolutionaries at San-Lauri on 30 June, 1409. The news of the victory arrived in Barcelona on 14 July, and was the occasion of great rejoicing, which soon gave place to mourning on the receipt of the news ten days later of the young King's death. Aragon was left without an heir to the throne, and Martin the Elder, whose wife had died in 1407, was compelled to seek another partner. On 17 September, 1409, his nuptials with Margarita de Pratz were celebrated in the Castle of Bellesquardo by Benedict XIII, and St. Vincent Ferrer said the Nuptial Mass.[1]   After the ceremony Benedict XIII, accompanied by St. Vincent, made a pilgrimage to the Sanctuary of Our Lady of Montserrat; from

but the street which has been made on their site is still called the *Calle de la Puerta del Angel*. The convent of St. Catherine, where our Saint studied in 1374, has also been destroyed, and its place is now occupied by a Fishmongers' Hall! (cf. Fages, "Histoire," p. 222; *seqq.* "Notes et Documents," pp. 149-50).

[1] Fages, "Histoire," pp. 227-28; "Notes et Documents," p. 151.

thence St. Vincent went to Manresa, famous a century later as the place where another glorious saint wrote the Spiritual Exercises—St. Ignatius of Loyola.[1]

On leaving Manresa, St. Vincent journeyed to Lerida, where he had already studied in the early days of his religious life. The large wooden barrier within which he walked on his journeys to protect himself from the people who pressed round him is still preserved in the Dominican Church there. He arrived at Lerida on 15 December, 1409, but hastened back to Barcelona, where the people were in a state of panic owing to the ravages of the plague. His presence calmed them; his exhortations stirred them to repentance; and with their repentance came the cessation of the plague.[2]

[1] St. Ignatius spent a year in the Dominican Convent of St. Peter Martyr at Manresa, under the guidance and instruction of the Prior, who was also his confessor, Guillem de Pellaros. At the end of the year, the Prior allowed him to retire to the Santa Cueva, but on condition that he presented himself once a week at the Convent. The heavy cross which the Founder of the Society of Jesus used to carry on his shoulders night after night through the cloisters of the Convent is still in the possession of the Dominicans. It bears the inscription in rude character: *Enecus a Lohola portabat hanc Crucem,* 1522. It was at the altar of St. Vincent Ferrer (not at the High Altar as Father Vita says), that St. Ignatius had the vision of the Blessed Trinity (Vita, S.J., " La Santa Cueva," *apud* Fages, " Notes et Documents," pp. 165-66; cf. " Histoire," pp. 229-31).

[2] Fages, " Histoire," p. 235.

Before he had left Genoa in 1406, the Florentines had sent an embassy beseeching him to visit
their city. The Saint was unable to do so, but replied
that he hoped one day to preach amongst them.
Another Dominican, Blessed Giovanni Dominici,
had preached at that very time in Florence, but the
people refused to hear him; and a third member
of the Order, a man worthy to stand beside St.
Vincent and Blessed Giovanni, was to startle the
Florentines by his thunderous eloquence, to receive
the homage of a people who regarded him as a
prophet and a Saint; and, finally, was to die at the
hands of this same people, who were not worthy
of him—Fra Girolamo Savonarola.   St. Vincent
thought to satisfy the desires of the Florentines in
1409, and had actually set out for Porta Venere
when a letter from Ferdinand of Castille forced
him to abandon his design.   He turned back,
preaching along the coast at Tarragona and Mont-
blanche, reconciling deadly enemies, acting as
judge in several disputes, and everywhere giving
palpable proof of his sanctity and the divine character of his work by the miracles he wrought.[1]

But a summons came from a quarter which the
Saint could not ignore.   Valencia, the city of his
birth, was in the throes of fratricidal war, to put an
end to which all efforts had hitherto proved
useless.   Even Benedict XIII had failed; and

[1] Cf. Fages, " Histoire," pp. 237-42; " Notes et Documents," pp. 160-62.

then the magistrates turned for help to the Preacher
and Wonder-Worker, the man in obedience to
whose words swords were sheathed, and hands
uplifted to strike were clasped in friendship with
those of their enemies.   They wrote to " Master
Vincent and their very dear Friend," craving his
help.   The first letter is dated 12 June, 1409,
and, on 28 August, another letter was forwarded.
But the Saint could come only very slowly, however
eager his desire, for there were souls to be saved
on the way.   A third letter was sent on 4
December ; then the news came that the Saint was at
Gaudesa, then at Tortosa, then Morella, where he
and his followers were provided with new garments
at the expense of the town.[1]   He remained at
Morella from 29 March until the end of May,
and shortly before his departure foretold the
death of Martin the Elder within eight days.   His
prophecy was fulfilled, and the King died at the
monastery of Valdoncelles on 31 May, 1410.[2].
Leaving Morella, St. Vincent came by Cati to
San Mateo,[3] preaching in several villages along
that almost impassable route through the moun-

[1] Fages, " Histoire," p. 252.

[2] *Ibid.*, p. 252 ; " Notes et Documents," p. 152.

[3] A sanctuary dedicated to the Saint is built at Caudiel,
near Cati.   The statue of *La Virgen del Niño Perdido*,
which the Saint gave to the Orphanage founded by him in
Valencia, is enshrined in this sanctuary (" Histoire," pp.
254-55).

tains.   The magistrates of Valencia were getting
impatient.   They wrote again on 25 April, and
a fourth time on 17 June, when they besought
St. Vincent to come for the Feast of St. John the
Baptist.   On 23 June, Valencia welcomed her
greatest son after an absence of fifteen years.   The
excitement was intense, but the enthusiasm may
better be imagined than described when the Saint
began to preach and when miracles in numbers
confirmed his preaching.   It was at Valencia that
he expelled the demon from the young woman who
in a time of peril had not demanded God's assistance, or made the sign of the Cross.[1]   Here it was
that he refused to give speech to the dumb woman
in order that her uncharitable thoughts might not
find utterance.[2]   And here also he converted two
Jewish criminals who were being led to death,
Israël Brunet and Isaac Conté.[3]   Two months
were spent by the Saint in Valencia, and it was at
this time, according to Teyxidor, that he founded
the Orphanage or *Collegio di Niños Perdidos*,
and set the University of Valencia on so solid a
footing as to deserve to be regarded as its founder.[4]

[1] "Acta Sanctorum," p. 503.   [2] *Ibid.*, pp. 501-2.
[3] Fages, " Histoire," p. 261 ; " Notes et Documents," p.
174.
[4] Established in 1374, the University was a failure, and
another effort was made in 1410.   St. Vincent took up the
cause and made it a success, and the University of Valencia
was erected on 11 October, 1411.   Becoming too small, a
new piece of land was acquired in 1417.   The solemn

The Orphanage was placed by the Saint under the care of the Beguins, a community which was certainly reorganized by him if indeed he was not its founder. This *Collegio di Niños* is still existing, and the boys, clothed in their white cassocks, take part in the choral offices in the Cathedral. Pope Urban VIII approved their rules, and the Orphanage possesses the Crucifix which St. Vincent used in his public processions.[1]

The Saint left his native city on 20 August, and journeyed southwards, preaching at Teulada, Alcira, and Denia. There he received an urgent summons from the Bishop of Valencia, on 29 September, to return and use his influence to prevent bloodshed owing to the refusal of Murviedro to allow the Governor of Valencia to enter the town. St. Vincent was judge and peacemaker once more ; and having settled the dispute he set out for Liria, where a miraculous well still bears witness to his beneficent visit, and the pulpit in the church tells us that the Saint preached from it in 1410, being then in his sixty-first year, while St. Louis

opening of the University did not take place until 1499, a circumstance which has caused some writers to deny that St. Vincent had anything to do with its foundation. Vidal y Mico, however, says it is certain that the Saint is the real founder of the University, and Teyxidor proves the fact in a conclusive manner (" Studios Antiquos e Modernos e Valencia," *apud* Fages, " Notes et Documents," pp. 178-79).

[1] Fages, " Histoire," pp. 269-70.

Bertrand preached from the same pulpit in 1571.[1]
He preached throughout the whole country of
Albyada, Thura, Consentaya, Fortuna, Avanilla,
and Elche, a country in the hands of the Moors,
but which became, and has remained ever since,
most fervently Christian in consequence of the
labours of St. Vincent.   Near Jativa, in the Castle
of Cavalls, Alphonsus Borgia was born.   He became Calixtus III, and canonized St. Vincent as
the Saint himself had prophesied.[2]   A letter from
the magistrates of Orihuela to the Bishop of Murcia,
Paul of Carthagena, dated 4 March, 1411, speaks
of the marvellous effects of the Saint's preaching.
Gambling, fortune-telling, blasphemy, and vice of
every kind had completely disappeared, and the re-
conciliations between those at enmity were universal.[3]

The year 1411 is remarkable in that St. Vincent
has left a record of his journeys which, incomplete
though it is, enables us to follow him step by step
and to obtain a knowledge of the distances traversed, and the sermons preached by him in his
boundless zeal for the souls of men.[4]   From

[1] Fages, "Histoire," pp. 272-73.   The date furnishes
another proof that the Saint was born in 1350.

[2] "Acta Sanctorum," p. 497; Fages, "Histoire," p. 276.

[3] Fages, "Histoire," p. 281-82; "Notes et Documents,"
p. 189.

[4] The MS. is preserved in the Library of the Patriarchate
at Valencia, and the record occupies pp. 193-95, in "Notes
et Documents".

Murcia in the south-east, where he remained from 29
January to 24 February, the Saint went to Lorca.
Returning to Murcia for Easter he set out immediately after the Feast and preached in the surrounding
towns, Molina, Ciessa, Jumilla, Hellim, Chinchilla,
Ciudad-Real, until he arrived at Toledo, where he
spent the month of July, going to Ocaña for the
Feast of St. Dominic.   At Illescas he fell seriously
ill on 12 August, and had to return to Toledo, where
he was compelled to remain for six weeks on account
of the fever which completely prostrated him.[1]
As soon as his health permitted him, he set out
again, and in Valladolid he preached thirty-six sermons, most of which were addressed to the Jews,
who were all-powerful there and in Toledo.   The
Jews had earned the bitter hatred of the people,
the poor in particular, by their exorbitant usury
and the permission which had been given them by
Henry III to come into possession of the property
of all those who were unable to pay the enormous
sums they demanded as interest.   St. Vincent obtained the repeal of this law, and urged the Queen
and the Infante Ferdinand to take steps to curb the
insolence and evil practices of their Jewish subjects.
He visited the Court at Ayllon, and while inspiring
all who beheld him with veneration and awe, he re-

---

[1] At Alcaraz and Moraleia, the Saint tells us in his record
he fell ill, and had to give up preaching for a time :
" propter infirmitatem meam que intervenit mihi "—by reason
of the illness which came upon me.

cognized in Ferdinand those qualities which should adorn every ruler—gentleness, broad-mindedness, and firmness.   These two men became friends at Ayllon, and it was chiefly owing to St. Vincent that Ferdinand of Castille ascended the throne of Aragon in the following year.[1]

[1] According to Vidal y Mico and the Bollandists it was in this year, 1411, that St. Vincent took possession of the Jewish Synagogue which became the Church of Santa Maria la Blanca.   Père Fages places the incident as having occurred in 1408 ("Histoire," pp. 193-94), though he says it is not improbable that it occurred in 1411.   We have seen how one writer speaks of this fact as a " desecration "; but it is well . to remember that the Jews are and have been as a body the sworn enemies of Jesus Christ and His Church.   The persecution of the Church in France, Italy, Spain, and Portugal to-day by Jewish Freemasons is merely the repetition of the persecution which they carried on in the fifteenth century.   Some writers, of course, would pardon every atrocity when the Catholic Church is the victim.

CHAPTER VI.

"THE ANGEL OF THE JUDGMENT."

WHEN St. Vincent left Ayllon in the beginning of the year he directed his steps southwards to Salamanca, preaching in various towns and villages along the way. In Zamora his preaching was signalized in a startling manner, as we shall see later. Part of February and March were devoted to the work of evangelizing the city of Salamanca where the two marvellous events which we shall now relate took place. They are both of them well authenticated. In Salamanca, as elsewhere, the Saint directed his attention to the conversion of the Jews, whom he regarded as the chief obstacles to the spread of Christianity. They had the control of the finances of the city at the time, as they have had and have control of the finances of other places ever since. Entering their Synagogue, crucifix in hand, St. Vincent began to preach to them. He employed all the powers of his eloquence. It was in vain: he could not move his hearers. Then he turned to the crucified image he held in his hand and besought Our Lord to soften the hearts of the Jews. His prayer was heard, and a shower of snow-white

48

crosses began to fall upon the Jews who were assembled. This prodigy moved those who had remained deaf to the pleading of the Saint. The
Jews were received into the Church, and their Synagogue became the Sanctuary of the Vera Cruz.[1]
"This was the Saint's first miracle in Salamanca," says Father Juan de Araya, "but it was
not his greatest nor his only miracle." The greatest
miracle here referred to is the one which gives the
title to this Chapter, when St. Vincent raised a
woman from death in confirmation of his claim to
be the Angel of the Apocalypse.

Preaching in the open space, now within the
garden of the Dominican Convent of St. Stephen
(or San Esteban) on a hillock named the Mount
of Olives, St. Vincent solemnly declared that he
was the Angel of the Judgment spoken of by
St. John the Evangelist in his Apocalypse.[2] An

---

[1] Fages, "Histoire," pp. 309-11; "Notes et Documents," pp. 207-11. The church was given to the Order of
Mercy in this same year, 1412, and a Latin inscription re-
calling the event was placed on the façade.

[2] xiv. 6: "And I saw another angel flying through the
midst of heaven, having the Eternal Gospel, to preach unto
them that sit upon the earth, and over every nation, and
tribe, and tongue, and people: Saying with a loud voice:
Fear the Lord, and give Him honour, because the hour of
His judgment is come". Our readers will remember that
the term Angel defines the office not the nature of these
beings, and means a messenger or herald. (Cf. the article
"Angel" by Father Hugh Pope, O.P., in "Catholic Ency-
clopedia," 1907, London, I, 476-81.)

immense concourse of people was present, and
the fathers of the Convent, many of them theologians of the Inquisition, were witnesses of the
declaration, which caused murmuring amongst the
audience. Startling as the words of St. Vincent assuredly were, his confirmation of his claim
was still more startling. A dead woman was being
brought to the Church of St. Paul hard by, at the
time of the sermon. St. Vincent ordered the
bearers to bring the corpse before him. Strong in
the strength of God the Saint adjured the dead
woman to testify whether his words were true or
not ; and before the eyes of all present the dead
woman came to life for a moment, bore witness to
the truth of the Saint's claim, then slept in death
once more, her mission accomplished. A cross
was raised on the spot where this occurrence took
place. A fresco in the Convent of San Esteban
represents the scene, and an inscription recounts
to all who care to read it the history of claim of
St. Vincent Ferrer and its miraculous confirmation.[1]

[1] Cf. Fages, " Histoire," pp. 311-19; Bayle, op. cit., p.
206. The Cross was in its place as late as 1901, and a Dominican father who visited San Esteban gave the writer of this
sketch a description of it. The Convent itself was the place
from which Columbus started on his voyage of discovery.
When all others had turned against him, Columbus found a
warm friend in the Dominican Bishop Diégo de Déza. The
University had given it against Columbus; but Diégo " and
his Dominicans, to their undying glory, were too enlightened
to acquiesce in the sentence of the professors " (" The Cities

It was thus that St. Vincent bore testimony to the mission he had received from Jesus Christ at Avignon, on 3 October, 1408. This mission was unique and without parallel in the history of the Church. Other preachers, Saints amongst the number, have roused sinners to repentance by their vivid portrayal of the Judgment; but St. Vincent's mission was as different and distinct from theirs as his preaching was diverse. To say that the Saint spoke of the approach of the Particular Judgment, is altogether to misunderstand his mission. He was the Apostle of the Last, and General Judgment, and it was the near approach of this Universal Judgment which he preached. Was he wrong, or did he prophesy falsely?

Two things must be considered in St. Vincent's mission: his claim to be the Angel of the Apocalypse, and his prophecy of the near approach of the Day of Wrath. It was to come "Soon, very soon, within a short time": *Cito, bene cito et valde breviter,* were the expressions which he used repeatedly. Regarding his claim to be considered the Angel of the Apocalypse, we must remember that he made it in the presence of those staunch guardians of the faith and of the Church, the fathers of San Esteban. They did not protest against the claim, for the miracle was an all-sufficient proof in

of Spain," by Ed. Hutton, p. 53; cf. "Les Dominicains et La Découverte de l'Amérique," by Père Mandonnet, O.P., Paris, 1893).

their eyes of the truth of the preacher's words. Furthermore, St. Vincent wrote to Benedict XIII to substantiate his claim to the title, and Benedict approved of it.[1] The Bull of Canonization compares St. Vincent to an " angel flying through the midst of heaven," and makes use of the very words of the Apocalypse in which St. John describes his vision. This passage has been incorporated in the Breviary Office for the feast of St. Vincent.[2] St. Louis Bertrand did not hesitate to say in a sermon that St. Vincent was the Angel foretold by the Evangelist ;[3] and Father Gonzalès Arriega applies to "St. Vincent Ferrer that Prince of Preachers," the words of the Apocalypse which we have quoted. Tradition, as we know, and the Church have sanctioned those pictures of the Saint which represent him with an Angel's wings, the Trumpet of the Judgment in his hand, and the text on which he preached so often —" Fear God, and give Him honour, for the day of His judgment is at hand ".[4] Since the Church has sanctioned and allowed the title which the Saint claimed to be his, no one, we venture to say, will dare to dispute it.

[1] Cf. " Histoire," pp. 322-25 ; " Notes et Documents," pp. 213-24.

[2] Cf. Fages, Vol. II, pp. 325-42, for the Bull of Canonization, and " Brev. Ord. Prod.," Die Va Aprilis.

[3] Fages, Vol. I, p. 325.

[4] For a list of early representations of St. Vincent Ferrer, we refer our readers to Fages, " Notes et Documents," pp. lviii-lx.

But St. Vincent foretold the near approach of the General Judgment; it has not come, though four centuries have elapsed since the prophecy was uttered. How, then, are we to reconcile the prophecy with its non-fulfilment? Does it not seem as if St. Vincent was in error? According to Père Fages, St. Vincent prophesied the approach of the Last Judgment in a conditional sense, as Jonas prophesied regarding the destruction of Niniveh;[1] and the final catastrophe was averted by the repentance of the nations in consequence of the prayers and preaching of the Saint.[2] While there is much to be said in favour of this opinion, we do not think it answers the case fully. There is no doubt that the widespread corruption of the time, the Schism, plague, and wars were regarded by many as signs of the approaching end of all things. Some of the early Fathers regarded the Fall of the Roman Empire as a presage of the Last Judgment; while the spiritual interpretation given by St. Gregory to the prophecy of Jesus Christ, that before the Son of Man should come to judge the world, the Sun should be darkened, the Moon should lose its light, the Stars should fall from heaven, and false Christs should appear,[3] seemed to have been completely realized in St. Vincent's time. The knowledge of Jesus Christ, the Sun of Justice, was no longer bright in the

[1] Jonas, III. 4. [2] "Histoire," Vol. I, pp. 336-41.
[3] St. Matthew, XXIV. 24, 29.

minds of men. The Church, the Moon reflecting
the light of that Sun, Jesus Christ, had lost her
light when there were three claimants to the
Papacy. The Stars, that is, the prelates and
pastors of the Church, were fallen from their
fervour and had become ambitious and worldly
place-seekers, numbered amongst those who "sit
upon the earth"; while false Christs had appeared
in the persons of Wickliff, Huss, and Jerome of
Prague.[1] More forcible still, the two signs which
are to usher in the time of the Last Judgment, viz.
the preaching of the Gospel throughout the world,
and the conversion of the Jews, seemed to have appeared when St. Vincent himself preached throughout
Europe and received 70,000 Jews into the Church.[2]

Now it is well to remember that prophecy is an
act, not a habitual state; that it is the outcome of
a Divine revelation; and that in this revelation there
is something explicitly revealed and something which
is the result of a secret instinct.[3] Furthermore, the
mind of the prophet is, in St. Thomas's language, a
"deficient instrument";[4] and though future events,
because they are known to God as they are in

[1] Cf. Fages, "Histoire," Vol. I, p. 326 *seqq.*

[2] *Ibid.*, p. 334. The "Acta Sanctorum" (p. 493), following Razzano, gives 25,000 Jews and 8000 Saracens converted by the Saint. The Jews themselves gave 200,000
as the number converted by St. Vincent.

[3] St. Thomas, "Summa Theologica," II[a]. II[a], Q.
CLXXI, Art. 1, 2, 5.

[4] *Ibid.*, Q. CLXIII, Art. 4.

themselves, are in consequence determined; yet in so far as they are dependent upon their immediate causes, they are mere contingencies. Moreover the prophet cannot always tell in which way they are made known to him, for sometimes the future is revealed as it is in itself, sometimes as dependent upon its immediate cause.[1] Hence the prophet, while absolutely certain regarding what has been explicitly revealed, since such revelation emanates from Primal and Essential Truth, is not certain in regard to those future events which have not been explicitly revealed. He may rely upon the secret instinct, and may be affected by the circumstances of the time in such wise as to deduce, by way of purely human reasoning, from the explicit revelation which he has received and which causes absolute certitude, certain conclusions for which he has received no warranty and which are not the subject-matter of prophecy. These deductions are merely human deductions, and as such they may be erroneous. If we apply these principles to St. Vincent's prophecy, we think we shall be able to give a truer explanation. He was enlightened by God, and received an explicit revelation to announce the approaching judgment—in God's own time, to whom there is neither past nor future, but who sees everything in an Eternal present. He had received a Divine command to preach the approach of the Judgment, as Legate *a latere Christi ;* but he

[1] St. Thomas, *Ibid.*, Art. 6, ad. 2m.

had not received any explicit revelation as to when the Judgment was to be. The universal decadence and corruption of the time, emphasized so strongly by the canons of the Council of Constance later, and by Pierre d'Ailly, Bishop of Cambrai;[1] the plague, Schism, wars, and famine; the preaching of the Gospel and the conversion of the Jews all pointed to the immediate approach of the Day of Judgment. St. Vincent was influenced by these signs; and from the explicit revelation which he had received, he concluded by way of human reasoning that the Day was close at hand when the Divine Judge should summon a corrupt and a corrupting world to hear the sentence He would pronounce upon it. This explanation seems more in keeping with St. Vincent's preaching, for if we mistake not, he never preached a conditional approach of the General Judgment. It harmonizes with two other prophecies of the Saint to which we have already referred. He foretold that Alphonsus Borgia should become Pope and should canonize him, and Alphonsus was only a boy at the time : and he also prophesied that Bernardine of Siena should be canonized before him, though St. Bernardine was only a youth when St. Vincent uttered his prophecy at Alexandria.[2] Both these pro-

---

[1] "Orat. in Matthæum ; " *apud* Fages, " Notes et Documents," pp. 211-12.

[2] Cf. Mortier, " Histoire des Maîtres Généraux, O.P." Vol. IV, pp. 53-57.

phecies were literally fulfilled. We are at liberty to choose either of the explanations given, and it should be remarked, as Père Fages tells us, that St. Antoninus attributed the postponement of the Last Judgment to the preaching of our Saint, basing his assertion on the words of St. Ambrose: "God will change his sentence if we but change our life".[1] Hence, concludes Père Fages, "God would have allowed the human race to fall into the abyss if another power, strong and mighty, had not prevented the catastrophe by setting humanity on the right path which led towards its real destiny. This power was the intervention of St. Vincent Ferrer, Prophet, Apostle, and Angel of the Judgment. He awakened the conscience of mankind by his preaching; brought men back from sin to the Feet of God; and reassured the world by proclaiming that man's repentance had saved it."[2]

[1] Novit Deus mutare sententiam, si tu noveris emendare delictum, "Histoire," pp. 339-40.

[2] *Ibid.*, p. 341.

CHAPTER VII.

"WHO SHALL BE KING?"

FROM Salamanca the Saint directed his steps towards the kingdom of Aragon, and in Segovia, where he arrived in May, 1412, the same enthusiasm and the same triumphs were witnessed as everywhere else. According to the historian of Segovia, his audience numbered 70,000 and sometimes 80,000 persons;[1] and one of the witnesses examined during the Process for St. Vincent's canonization affirmed that *all* the Jews who attended his sermons were received into the Church. In three months, says another witness, Vincent Ferrer converted 25,000 Jews in Castile alone. In Villalba, during the public processions, the people still halt before the little shuttered window of a house which is inhabited by a family of the glorious and historic name of the Saint. A lamp burns before the window, and the people sing the *Te Deum*. It was from this window St. Vincent preached during his visit to the place.[2] Near Plascensia, the envoy of the united Parliaments of Catalonia, Aragon,

[1] Colemanarès, *apud* Fages, "Histoire," p. 342.
[2] Fages, "Histoire," p. 347.

58

and Valencia, Michel de Ribas, came to meet the
Saint to request his immediate presence at Caspe,
where a successor to the throne of Aragon, left
vacant by the deaths of Martin the Elder and
Martin the Younger, was to be chosen.   Martin the
Younger had left a natural son, Count de Luna,
but he could not succeed to Aragon as he had
been legitimized to succeed to the kingdom of
Sicily only;[1] and the thoughts of the dying King
at Valdoucelles turned to his nephew, Ferdinand,
Infante of Castile.   But the Count de Urgell,
another claimant, urged on by his mother, claimed
the right to rule.[2]   When Ferdinand heard the
wishes of the dying King he went to Saragossa from
Antequera, where he had completely vanquished
the Moorish King of Grenada,[3] and issued a pro-
clamation in which he stated that, "as the nearest
relative of Martin, he would accept, when the time
came, succession to the Kingdom of Aragon with
all its lands and possessions".   The Parliament of
Catalonia imposed silence on Urgell, and asked
Aragon and Valencia to send plenipotentiaries to
discuss the situation.   But dissension arose in the
Parliament itself, and in 1411 the Archbishop of
Saragossa was foully murdered by Antonius de

[1] "Couronne d'Aragon," *apud* Fages, "Notes et Documents," p. 227.

[2] *Ibid.;* cf. "Histoire," p. 351.

[3] Cayetano Rosell: "Chronique des Rois de Castille,"
Vol. II, p. 320; *apud* Fages, "Histoire," p. 352.

Luna, an adherent of Urgell, because he had declared that as long as he lived he would oppose Urgell's claims to the throne.[1] Urgell raised an army. Ferdinand protested against this action, and Urgell replied that he merely desired to protect himself. Then Ferdinand levied his troops and entered Aragon. The Parliament of Catalonia held its sessions at Tortosa ; Aragon assembled its Parliament at Alcañiz ; and two opposing Parliaments of Valencia held their sittings at Vinoraz and Trayquera respectively. Dissensions increased ; Benedict XIII offered his assistance in vain ; and then it was that "the desire took possession of all parties to ask the blessed Master Vincent Ferrer to come to their assistance, as the one man who could bring about an understanding amongst those who were on the verge of bloodshed ".[2]

There were six claimants: John of Pratz ; Alphonsus of Gandia ; Frederick, Count of Luna— the natural son of Martin the younger; James, Count of Urgell; Louis of Anjou, Count of Calabria ; and Ferdinand, Infante of Castile ; but the chief were Urgell and Ferdinand. The Cortes of Aragon, Catalonia, and Valencia chose nine Judges in February, 1412. Those of Aragon were Dominic Ram, Bishop of Huesca; Francis d'Aranda, a

---

[1] "Chronique des Rois," p. 337; *apud* Fages, " Histoire," p. 354.

[2] Zurita: "Annales de la Couronne d'Aragon," Liv. XI, Ch. XL. ; *apud* Fages, " Histoire," p. 355.

Carthusian monk of Porta-Cæli; and Berengarius Bardaxinus. Pedro Saggariga, Archbishop of Tarragona, Guillem de Valesca, and Bernard de Gualbes, represented Catalonia; while Valencia chose Boniface Ferrer, General of the Carthusians, St. Vincent Ferrer, and Ginés Rabaxa. "All were men of excellent qualities," says Zurita, "but the man who shone like the sun amongst them all by reason of his sanctity, was Father Vincent Ferrer. Each felt sure that with such a guide none would stray from the paths of truth and justice." La Fuente in his " Histoire Générale d'Espagne," speaks in exactly the same terms.[1] The town of Caspe between Tortosa and Alcañiz was chosen as the seat of the deliberations; and the conduct of Urgell and Ferdinand is noteworthy. The former sought to make an impression by the splendour of his retinue; Ferdinand, on the contrary, withdrew from the vicinity.

St. Vincent was one of the last to arrive, but it was evident from the very beginning that the responsibility of the whole proceedings would fall upon his shoulders. On the appointed day, the nine judges having heard Mass and received Holy Communion, swore on the Holy Gospels and the Crucifix "to proceed without delay to elect a King as seemed good in the sight of God, their conscience, and according to justice; and that they would not reveal their intentions or their deliberations, or

[1] *Apud* Fages, "Histoire," p. 359.

those of their fellow-judges before the day fixed for
the publication of their decision ".[1]   When this
was done St. Vincent preached on the text : " Let
there be one fold and one Shepherd," and "it was
a foregone conclusion," says a writer, "that the
verdict of this man would be given in accordance
with truth and justice ".

The discussions occupied thirty days, "and
when the different advocates had nothing further
to say," as an old chronicler states, "the judges
proceeded to elect a King ".   The question was
grave and the moment was a solemn one, in that
the decision was certain to affect the whole penin-
sula.   Urgell was insistent that the question of succession should not be left to the decision of a few,
since it belonged by right of birth and conquest to
one family, and that common sense as well as justice
pointed him out as the man who ought to succeed
to the throne, especially since Martin the Elder had
appointed him Lieutenant-General of his Kingdom.
The claims of the other four were not strong enough
to cause much difficulty, and the judges found
themselves called upon to decide between Urgell
and Ferdinand.   All eyes were fixed on St. Vincent.   He understood the desires of his fellow-
judges, and after a moment's recollection wrote his
decision.

"I, Brother Vincent Ferrer of the Order of

[1] Cf. The Oath in " Notes et Documents," p. 232 ; and
" Histoire," p. 357.

Preachers, Master of Theology, one of the Judges chosen by the Parliaments, affirm and decide to the best of my ability, that the Parliaments mentioned, the Subjects and Vassals of the Crown of Aragon, owe allegiance to the Illustrious and Puissant Lord, Ferdinand, Infante of Castile, grandson of Pedro King of Aragon of happy memory, the father of the highly esteemed late King Martin, as being their nearest male relative born in lawful wedlock. And I declare before God and my own conscience that all should regard the said Ferdinand as their true King and Lord.

"In witness whereof I sign this decision with my own hand and affix thereto my seal.

"FR. VINCENT FERRER, Preacher."

It is noteworthy that although St. Vincent was eighth on the list of judges he voted first. His decision was accepted by the Bishop of Huesca, by Boniface Ferrer, Bernard de Gualbes, Berengar de Bardaxi, and Francis d'Arranda. The Archbishop of Tarragona was divided in his opinions between Urgell and the Duke of Gandia. Guillem de Valseca gave the preference to Urgell as also did Pedro Bertrand; but as the Parliaments had decided that a majority of two-thirds was sufficient if representatives of each Parliament were included in the majority, Ferdinand of Castile was declared to have been elected. This was on 24 June, 1412.[1]

[1] "Histoire," pp. 357-65; "Notes et Documents," pp. 233-39; "Acta Sanctorum," p. 495; cf. "Catholic Ency-

On 29 June, the Bishop of Huesca celebrated Mass in the presence of the judges, the ambassadors of the three kingdoms, the nobility and people. St. Vincent preached on the text: "Let us rejoice and be glad and give glory to God, for the marriage of the Lamb is at hand:" and on the conclusion of his sermon, published the result of the election which decided that the Crown of Aragon should rest on the head of "the Most Illustrious, Most Excellent, and Most Puissant Lord and Prince, Ferdinand, Infante of Castile". The judges acclaimed the new King; the people followed suit; and thus the Kingdoms of Aragon and Castile were united. There were some dissentient voices nevertheless, for the Count de Urgell had many followers. But on the following day St. Vincent preached another sermon in which, having traced the new King's descent and praised him in warmest terms, he begged the malcontents not to be led astray by irresponsible people, but to accept in good part what had come about through God's Divine Will.

The choice of Ferdinand realized the fullest hopes of those who had elected him; and the subsequent career of the man in whom St. Vincent Ferrer recognized those qualities which should be found in every ruler confirmed the foresight and

clopædia," Vol. III, " Castile ": the writer, Father Ramon Avado, S.J., makes no mention of St. Vincent Ferrer in this article.

bore witness to the perspicacity of the Saint. The
"Compromise of Caspe" as it is called, has been
severely criticized even in our own time; yet despite
the unwillingness of certain men to approve of any
measure in which the Church and a Saint took part,
Vincent Ferrer is deserving of the title given him
by many more broad-minded and more generous
men—*Pater Patriæ*—the Father of his Country.
It was his influence which carried most weight in
the election; and it was the election of Ferdinand
which put an end to the dissension and strife at the
time.[1]

[1] The documents are given in "Notes et Documents," pp.
226-49, while a critical examination of the *Compromissio* is
given in the "Histoire," Vol. I, pp. 376-419.

CHAPTER VIII.

"IN LABOUR AND PAINFULNESS," 1412-1416.

As was to be expected, the Count de Urgell did
not accept the decision of Caspe without a protest.
He swore vengeance against St. Vincent; and on
a rising ground between Caspe and Peñalba a
stone cross marks the spot where the Count and
his followers lay in wait for the Saint as he
journeyed to Valencia. He rushed at St. Vincent,
calling him all kind of opprobrious epithets, but
St. Vincent quietly answered: "It is you who are
the wretch, for on such a day, in such a place, and
at such an hour you murdered your brother!"
The Count fled. No one had known of the
murder except himself. St. Vincent continued his
journey to Alcañiz, and it was from this place that
he wrote to Benedict XIII concerning his teach-
ings on the Judgment. Benedict was satisfied
with the explanation given by St. Vincent in his
letter of 29 July, 1412. Once again the old story
of triumph was repeated. The Jews in Alcañiz and
the surrounding districts embraced the true faith at
the preaching of the Saint. Their Synagogue became the Church of the Incarnation; one of the
Cathedral bells was called after him; and amongst

its most precious treasures were the Saint's crucifix, pulpit, vestments, and a copy of the "Summa" of St. Thomas with St. Vincent's marginal notes.[1]

According to Arénys, St. Vincent preached in Barcelona from 21 July to 26 August, 1412. His intention, we can readily surmise, was to urge the people to accept Ferdinand's election, and that he was successful in his efforts may be learned from the reception given to the King on his State entry into Barcelona on 28 November. A chapel here, a hermitage there, mark the footsteps of the Apostle, who is still the object of the loving veneration of the people in the country districts. He went to meet the King at Lerida in October, and the wonderful effects of his preaching are noted by Quintanis, the King's physician. Old feuds were forgotten. Old enemies became friends, and peace and concord reigned supreme. The halls of the University were deserted, many of the graduates and students giving up their studies to follow the Saint.[2]

We have said that St. Vincent was on his way to Valencia when he encountered Urgell; it was in answer to an invitation from the magistrates who, on 25 June, wrote to request him to finish the good work he had begun. In order to hasten his steps the

---

[1] Fages, "Histoire," Vol. II, pp. 7-9; "Notes et Documents," pp. 248-49. The "Summa" is now at Saragossa. The pulpit was placed in the new church and an Indulgence of 200 days is granted to all who pray before the image of the Saint. The other relics have long since disappeared.

[2] *Ibid.*, pp. 12-13.

magistrates wrote to Benedict XIII on the same day.[1]
St. Vincent arrived at Valencia on 29 November,
received "as if he were a king," says Diago. Two
months were spent in the city, and on this occasion
St. Vincent proved himself to be a man of business
as well as of prayer, for he placed the finances of
Valencia on a solid basis. He laboured in the
districts surrounding the city, and on 11 February,
1413, the magistrates wrote again asking him not
to fail to be present when the King paid his first
visit to Valencia; a week later they wrote to request
him to preach during the Lent.[2] When the Saint
arrived on 4 March, amid scenes of wildest rejoicing, a Franciscan Bishop who had met him at Perpignan, Francis Ximenes, said to him in his own
dialect: "*Frare Vicent, que fa la bufa?* Father
Vincent, how fares pride?" "It comes and goes,"
replied the Saint, "but does not stay, thank God."[3]
Miracles innumerable were wrought by him, two of
which are perpetuated by Spanish proverbs. "She
needs the assistance of St. Vincent," is said of a
woman who has no claims to be considered hand-
some, in allusion to the Saint having restored peace
between a husband and wife when the husband
had created disturbance by taunting his wife with
her ugliness. "Drink of the water of Master Vincent," is told to quarrelsome people, because the

[1] Fages, "Histoire," Vol. II, pp. 16-17; "Notes et
Documents," pp. 250-52.

[2] *Ibid.*, p. 20; "Notes et Documents," pp. 253-54.

Notes et Documents," p. 255.

Saint is said to have cured an ill-tempered dame by sending her to the Convent to get a jug of water from the well. When her husband began to nag, she was to take a mouthful of the water and *keep it in her mouth!* The remedy was most efficacious: it might be tried more frequently even now! The Convent of Valencia where the Saint stayed during this visit had been, as we have already seen, his home in the early years of his Dominican life, and now he was to bid farewell to it for ever. Not without a blessing though: "It shall always be the home of saints," he said, and time has confirmed the prophecy. On 23 April, St. Vincent preached his last sermon in Valencia, and three days later he left his native city never more to return.[1]

Ferdinand had written in February to ask for a Father to preach the Lent in Barcelona. He wrote on 12 April to request the Saint to meet him at Tortosa, where he hoped to treat with Benedict XIII regarding the cessation of the Schism, to bring about which, he, "as a Catholic King, was determined to do all in his power".[2] The next day he wrote another letter begging St. Vincent to preach throughout Catalonia, and the Saint, who did not arrive in Barcelona until 26 August, stayed but a short time there, for Ferdinand had been compelled to march against Urgell who, in company with the Duke of Clarence, was striving to

[1] "Histoire," p. 25.
[2] "Notes et Documents," p. 265.

stir up the country against the King.[1]   The Saint
embarked on 30 August for the Balearic Islands in
company with the Bishop of Majorca, Louis de
Pratz.   From his arrival at Palma on 1 September,
he preached all through these islands, which still
retain traces of his ministry, embarking again on
22 February and sailing for Tortosa, where he
arrived on 25 February.[2]   A conference of Jewish
Rabbis was held at Tortosa early in the year 1414.
St. Vincent composed his classic treatise against the
Jews for the occasion, and after sixty-nine meet-
ings, fourteen out of the sixteen Rabbis were received into the true Church.[3]   This was followed
by a general conversion of the Jews of the districts
around Tortosa, and with their conversion there
came about a widespread social improvement.[4]
Four other letters from Ferdinand to St. Vincent
were written at this time.   In the fourth letter the
King asks his advice concerning the miracle which
occurred at Guadalaxara ; and in June we find the
Saint taking part in the festival of *Corpus Christi*
at Daroca, where the blood-stained Hosts were

---

[1] " Histoire," p. 29 ; " Notes et Documents," p. 266.

[2] A detailed account of St. Vincent's missions in the
islands is given by Teyxidor, " Noticias de San Vicente ";
apud Fages, " Notes et Documents," pp. 268-74.

[3] " Histoire," p. 44 ; " Notes et Documents," pp. 279-80.
The two who were not converted were Albo and, strangely
enough, Ferrer.

[4] De Moner y de Siscar, " Historia de Tamarit"; *apud*
Fages, " Histoire," p. 46.

and are still the objects of a believing people's worship. From Daroca the Saint travelled to Morella where an astounding miracle which we shall speak of later took place. It was at Morella too that Benedict XIII discussed the question of the Schism with Ferdinand and St. Vincent. The conferences lasted fifty days, but Peter de Luna proved as obstinate as ever, and refused to abdicate, though the other two Pontiffs had agreed to do so if he yielded.[1] A well blessed by the Saint, which is always abundant even when all the other streams and wells of the place are dry, remains to-day fresh and limpid, a perpetual reminder of St. Vincent's labours at Morella.[2]

From November until the Easter of 1415, as we learn from one of his sermons, St. Vincent laboured in Saragossa. A proof of the success of his missions in Aragon is furnished by Zurita, who informs us that during this visit of the Saint to the Kingdom of Aragon, 3000 Jews were baptized.[3] Troli discovered a detailed account of a visit paid by the Saint to Bologna, from the pen of one Alessandro Machiavelli. According to this writer, St. Vincent visited Bologna in 1415; but there are no records to support Machiavelli's statements, which are probably the outcome of a lively imagination.[4] St.

[1] "Histoire," p. 56.   [2] *Ibid.*, pp. 57-58.
[3] Annals," Liv. XII, C. 45; *apud* Fages, "Histoire," p. 64.
[4] Cf. "Notes et Documents," pp. 285-92. The same Machiavelli presented two Saints to the Church, a Carmelite and a Dominican. They never had any existence outside

Vincent preached in Graus in June, 1415, and gave another crucifix to the church there. A Confraternity of the *Santo Crist* was established, and each year a triduum is held in honour of St. Vincent and the *Santo Crist* on 13, 14 and 15 September. The Saint preached in Barbastro towards the end of June, and proceeded to Ainça, where the fervour and enthusiasm of the people was such that the magistrates had to escort the Apostle through the streets to protect him.[1] At Cervera, where he stayed one night, the Saint was consoled by a vision of St. Dominic who conversed familiarly with him as a father would do with a well-loved Son. The voices brought the other religious on the scene, for it was most irregular to speak during the time of the Great Silence, and in this way was the vision made known.[2] He laboured in and around Conflans during August, and not far from the town fed 4000 men, not counting women and children, with seven loaves and a few fishes.[3]

But his labours in Spain were ended. Ferdinand was anxious to do all in his power to put an end to the

the imagination of the man who "evolved them from his inner consciousness".

[1] " Histoire," p. 73.   [2] *Ibid.*, p. 75.

[3] *Ibid.*, p. 76. On another occasion St. Vincent worked a similar miracle while preaching in Catalonia, when some 2500 persons, as Antonio Roca, one of the number, testified, were fed by " visitors who brought an abundance of food and drink ". These miracles have obtained liturgical sanction by being mentioned in the first Responsory of the Third Nocturne in the Office of St. Vincent.

Schism, and at his request St. Vincent embarked at Barcelona for Nice, never again to set foot in Spain.

The confusion at the time was extreme. The "Council" of Pisa in 1409 had intensified it by electing Alexander V as Pope, and so the Christian world was scandalized by the spectacle of three claimants to the Papacy. Alexander died ten months later, and Balthazzar Cossa was chosen in his place, taking the name of John XXIII. Gregory XII, the legitimate Pontiff, was an exile. John XXIII reigned at Rome. Benedict XIII, as obstinate as ever, asserted his claims and would not hear of any compromise. In November, 1414, John XXIII, compelled by the Emperor Sigismund, had opened the Council of Constance, which solemnly deposed him and demanded the abdication of Gregory XII and Benedict XIII. In May, 1415, Ferdinand wrote to St. Vincent to meet him at Collioure, but falling dangerously ill at Valencia he begged the Saint to proceed to Perpignan, where they would discuss the steps to be taken to ensure the union of the Church with Benedict XIII. St. Vincent arrived at Perpignan towards the end of August and began to use all his tact and powers of persuasion to make Benedict yield. Gregory XII had already signified his intention of resigning, and Benedict therefore was the sole obstacle in the way. But all the efforts of St. Vincent proved useless; Peter de Luna would not give in, and once again, as at Avignon sixteen years previously, the Saint fell so seriously ill that his life was despaired of.

Stubborn to the last, Benedict XIII fled to Peñis-
cola, whither an embassy was sent by Ferdinand to
try and obtain his consent to the proposed abdication. Again he refused; he would not abdicate.
We must not forget that in the eyes of St. Vincent
and Ferdinand, Benedict XIII was the true Pope,
hence their difficulties and embarrassing position.
But at last, when all efforts had proved unavailing,
Ferdinand asked St. Vincent to decide the question
finally. St. Vincent replied that since Benedict
XIII had resisted all attempts to procure the
union that was so necessary, and since his conduct
gave scandal to all the faithful, they were justified
in withdrawing their obedience to Benedict. This
decision was confirmed by the assembly of Bishops
convened by Ferdinand and representing the
obedience of Avignon. On 6 January, 1416, the
Feast of the Epiphany, St. Vincent sang Mass,
and preached to some 10,000 persons. After the
sermon, he read in the presence of the King, Ambassadors, and people, the act by which all those
who had been of the Avignon obedience withdrew
their allegiance to Benedict. The Emperor was
notified of this; and the Fathers of the Council of
Constance sang a *Te Deum* in thanksgiving. Gerson wrote to St. Vincent: "But for you this union
could never have been accomplished".

The Schism was at an end.[1]

[1] Cf. Fages, "Histoire," pp. 79-121; "Notes et Documents," pp. 293-324; Pastor, op. cit., pp. 199-201; Bayle,
op. cit., p. 251 *seqq.*

CHAPTER IX.

THE EVENING OF LIFE. 1416–1419.

THE later journeys of St. Vincent, his success, the miracles which he wrought and the conversions effected by his preaching, are well authenticated; and this is due not only to the Process of Canonization but also to the records which were kept by the various municipalities of the places in which he laboured. We can follow him step by step after the Conferences in Perpignan and Narbonne, in 1416, to Vannes where he died three years later, and everywhere we find a repetition of his earlier triumphs, of astounding miracles and marvellous conversions; and of a life which was lived in closest communion with God.

It is quite certain that our Saint received an urgent summons to the Council of Constance. It was Ferdinand's desire that St. Vincent should take part in the Council; and on Ferdinand's death on 2 April, 1416, his son, Alphonsus V, renewed his father's wish. Sigismund had expressed the same wish; and the letter which Gerson wrote, and to which the Bishop of Cambrai added a postscript, urging St. Vincent to come to the Council, is still

extant.[1]   But St. Vincent did not attend the
Council in person, though he received a deputation
of theologians at Dijon and settled a knotty question which they, on behalf of the Council, proposed
to him.[2]   Yet though St. Vincent was not person-
ally present at the Council his influence was felt
very strongly, since those assembled at Constance
knew well that the union and peace of the Church
had been brought about chiefly by him.   If the
power of Benedict XIII had not been broken, and
if Spain had not renounced all allegiance to him,
the Council could never have been so successful
because it would not have been so united.   Benedict XIII was fully aware that his day was over
when Vincent Ferrer withdrew the support of his
name and sanctity.   St. Vincent led the way.   The
other adherents of Benedict followed the Saint's
example, and when Benedict was left alone the last
obstacle to union was removed.

After the Conferences at Perpignan and Narbonne
St. Vincent set out for Toulouse, travelling through
Narbonne, Beziers, and Castelnaudary.   France
was to receive the last ministrations of this wonderful apostle.   He entered Toulouse in the evening
of Friday in Passion-Week, seated on the ass which
his years and infirmities had rendered a necessary
mode of conveyance.   Once more we are face to

[1] Cf. " Histoire," pp. 112-19; "Notes et Documents,"
pp. 322-24.
[2] " Histoire," p. 118.

face with the manifestly supernatural; with the gift
of tongues, miracles innumerable, and extraordinary
conversions.   The Archbishop testified afterwards
that, although the Saint was an old man, worn by
watchings, fasts, and labours, once he began to
preach -his face became transfigured.   He seemed
to be a young man, full of vigour, and gifted with a
powerful and ringing voice.[1]   The enthusiasm of
the people was unparalleled.   All business was sus-
pended : shops were shut, the Law-Courts and the
University were closed.   The Cathedral could not
hold the enormous crowds, and St. Vincent preached
in the public square outside the Cathedral to an
audience which not only filled the square and the
houses, but which found a somewhat dangerous
position on the roofs round about.   On Good
Friday it was estimated that at least 30,000 people
were present at the Sermon on the Passion ; and
Jean Regis, the Rector of the Cathedral, has recorded that when the Saint cried out in his sermon
on the Last Judgment : *Arise ye dead and come to
judgment*, it seemed as if in truth he was the Angel
of the Judgment himself.   His voice rang out with
such terrifying power that the people flung themselves on the ground crying for mercy and pardon.[2]
Each evening, according to the invariable custom,

[1] Cf. " Histoire," pp. 149-52.   Other witnesses bear testimony to this youthful appearance of the Saint when preaching.   Cf. " Histoire," pp. 166-67, 181.

[2] " Histoire," p. 153.

there was a Procession of Penitents.   Then there
might be seen careless, wilful University students
walking side by side with grave and learned professors, barefooted and with uncovered shoulders
that bled from the strokes of the scourge which
they wielded with no sparing hand.[1]

From Toulouse St. Vincent travelled through
Muret, Carmaing, Castres, Albi, Galliac, and Cordes,
arriving at Najac on 17 June, amidst the frenzied
acclamations of the people who hailed him as the
people of Jerusalem hailed Our Lord.   He preached
at Saint-Flour and Puy, reaching the latter city on
3 October, and the remainder of the year was devoted to missions in Auvergne.   Then he proceeded
to Lyon and Mâcon, and when he had laboured
in the surrounding districts, he travelled through
Bourg, Tournus, Rochefort, and Auxonne to Poligny,
where he met St. Colette.[2]   St. Vincent, however,
had really undertaken this journey in order to meet
and confer with St. Colette, as he acknowledged
to Père de la Balme.[3]   The short conference at
Poligny was not enough to satisfy either St. Vincent or St. Colette, and so he followed St. Colette
to Besançon, where he arrived on 4 June, 1417.[4]
His mission lasted three weeks and he preached six

[1] " Histoire," p. 159.
[2] " Année Dominicaine," pp. 205-6; " Histoire," pp.
193-94.
[3] " Vita Sæ Colettæ," 1520; apud " Histoire," p. 190.
[4] " Histoire," p. 189; " Acta Sanctorum " die IVᵃ. Julii.

times to St. Colette and her nuns.   In the Convent he saw and venerated the gold cross studded
with fine pearls which Our Divine Lord had given
to His Spouse ; and St. Vincent left to the Saint
in memory of his visit the Crucifix which he usually
held in his hand, or placed in the pulpit while
preaching.   During one of the interviews between
these two servants of God, St. Colette was wrapt
in ecstasy, and afterwards told her saintly friend
that God would call him to receive the reward of
his labours within two years ; and, furthermore, that
he should die in France, not in Spain.[1]

On leaving Besançon, St. Vincent went to Dijon
and then to Chambéry where he laid the founda-
tion-stone of a Dominican Priory on 22 January,
1418.   On his way from Dijon he paid a visit to
the famous Cistercian Monastery of Clairvaux.
The ranks of the monks had been decimated by
the plague and many of them were in a dying state
when St. Vincent arrived.   He blessed the Monastery and the dying monks.   The plague ceased,
and the sick recovered immediately.[2]   His stay at
Chambéry was very brief, and he probably returned
by the same route, preaching at Angers and arriving at Nantes in 8 February.   Here he remained
ten days and then travelled through Savenay,
Fegréac, and Redon to Vannes, where his reception

[1] "Histoire," p. 191 *seqq.*; "Année Dominicaine," pp.
210-12.
[2] "Histoire," pp. 198-200.

was worthy of the Ages of Faith. The Bishop,
Amaury de la Notte, the Chapter, priests and
people came some distance to meet him and
brought him in triumph to the city; but just outside the gates of Vannes another welcome awaited
him. The blind and deaf, the lame, the sick and
ailing people had gathered on each side of the
road. They cried out as did the lepers of old to
be healed of their infirmities, and St. Vincent,
moved beyond measure, blessed them. And lo!
the sightless eyes saw, the lame leaped up, and
the dumb spoke, and the cries of the stricken were
changed into hymns of thanksgiving as they called
down God's benediction on His servant who had
healed them by a word.[1]

Three weeks were occupied in preaching in and
around Vannes, and on 29 March he set out to
labour in the other villages and towns of Brittany.
Theix, Josselin, Ploermel, and Rennes were visited;
and, receiving an invitation at Rennes from Henry
V of England to preach in Normandy, St. Vincent
proceeded to Caen, where Henry held his Court.[2]
The old chronicler speaks of the astonishment of
the King and his Court when they heard the Saint
" preaching, as it were in the language of each one
present," but their astonishment gave place to awe
when St. Vincent healed Guillaume de Villiers,

[1] " Histoire," pp. 214-16; " Année Dominicaine," pp.
214-15.

[2] " Histoire," p. 223; " Année Dominicaine," p. 215.

before their eyes.   The youth had been stricken dumb as a child, had refused all nourishment, and had become totally paralysed.   His brother gave evidence that even when beaten with rods until the blood came, Guillaume gave no sign of conscious-ness.   The Saint made the sign of the cross over the boy, who was instantly cured.[1]   Everywhere St. Vincent went, through Normandy, says Jean Ruault, he was prodigal of his miracles.   We may well believe it.   His stay there was necessarily short, and it was equally necessary to strengthen the faith of the people.   This he accomplished by means of the miracles which he wrought so lavishly.   They were the divine seal upon his mission; proofs un-assailable that he was guided by God.

We possess no definite dates of the Saint's labours in Normandy.   We know that he preached in Saint-Lô, Bayeux, Avranches, and Coutances; that he was at Dinan in June, at Saint-Brieuc in July, and that he returned to Brittany after preaching in Dol.[2]   Ten days were spent at Dinan, and then St. Vincent went to Jugon, Lamballe,—where the lady in whose house he stayed beheld his room lighted up with supernatural light—Montcour, and Saint-Brieuc.   Although we lose trace of our Saint dur-ing several months at this period, it is most prob-able that he went to Lesneven from Saint-Brieuc, travelling through Pontivy, Rostreneven, Carhaix,

---

[1] " Histoire," p. 227.

[2] *Ibid.*, p. 225; " Année Dominicaine," p. 215.

Heunebout, Quimperlé, Quimper, Port l'Abbé, Concarneau, and Chateaulin.   Mgr. de Lezelenc states that the Cathedral of Quimper—certainly the towers and the Chapel of Folgoet—were built by the followers of St. Vincent.[1]   Our Saint remained fifteen days at Morlaix, and continued his journey to La Chèze, La Trinite, Josselin, and Redon ; then at the request of the Bishop he preached during the Advent of 1418 at Nantes.[2]

[1] "Histoire," pp. 242-48.   The Story of the Fool whose only words were " Ave Maria," and over whose grave the lily, bearing the same words on its leaves, sprang up, is beautifully told by Alfred Austin in " A Breton Legend " (cf. " Carmina Mariana," by Orby Shipley.   First Series, pp. 33-35).   The Chapel of Folgoet—Fool's Wood—is built over the " Fool's " Grave.

[2] " Histoire," pp. 254-60 ; " Année Dominicaine," p. 216. Nantes possesses the Rosary given by St. Vincent Ferrer to Jeanne, Duchess of Brittany, and bequeathed by her to Blessed Frances d'Amboise.   " It is a five decade Rosary, strung on strong flaxen cord without knots.   The smaller beads being of the size of a pea, the *Paters* larger and slightly grooved.   The cross is composed of five beads. Possibly this gave rise to the custom of reciting the *Creed, Our Father*, and three *Hail Mary's* before beginning the Rosary proper " (Fages, " Histoire," p. 263).   Is this a proof of the Dominican origin of the Rosary ?   Blessed Frances was one of the strongest supporters of B. Alan de la Roche in *re-establishing* the Rosary Confraternities.   At Dinan the Dominican Convent was begun in 1216 and dedicated in 1224, through the generosity of Alain de Lanvallay who heard St. Dominic preach the Rosary.   Alain himself became an Apostle of the Rosary, and in the " Entrennes Dinnaises," which are based on the early records of the Convent, we are

The Saint was exhausted from his labours, so weak, indeed, that some of the Spaniards who were amongst his followers begged him to return to Spain that he might die in his native land.   St. Vincent smilingly consented and the party set out from Nantes by night so as not to distress the warm-hearted people.   But when day broke they found themselves once more before the gates of the city, and knew that God had willed it so.   "It is God's will that I shall die in Brittany," said the Saint.

The prophecy of St. Colette was to be fulfilled.[1]

told that: " Tiphanie Raguenel, wife of Bertrand Duguesclin, is buried in the *Rosary Chapel* of the Convent Church ". It is somewhat strange to read that there is no vestige of proof to show that St. Dominic founded the Rosary.   Such criticism at this time of day is cheap.   It is also incorrect ; for despite the determined efforts which have been made to disprove the Dominican tradition, which, be it said, has been handed down by the Church, that tradition remains intact (cf. "St. Dominic and the Rosary," by Father Wilfrid Lescher, O.P., London, 1902).

[1] Cf. " Histoire," p. 260 ; "Année Dominicaine," p. 227.

CHAPTER X.

THE CROWN OF GLORY.

ST. VINCENT'S work was almost finished. His day was nearly done, and it was a spent and weary man who returned to Vannes at the beginning of 1419. He lodged with a family named Dreulin, yet dying though he was, stricken down on the field of battle, he would continue his labours until the very last. He sang Mass and preached every day, eating but little and never touching meat. Those who loved him tried hard to prevent the inevitable. They surrounded him with every care in the vain hope of prolonging the life of so saintly an Apostle and so apostolic a Saint—for they called him "St. Vincent" long before his death. In their anxiety they thought once more to take him home to Spain, this time by sea, and actually embarked at a spot which is still called *Porte St. Vincent*. The dying man allowed his friends to have their way, though he knew it was useless. He became so seriously ill as soon as they had set sail that they were compelled to return to Vannes, and Vincent Ferrer re-entered the city to the joyous pealing of the bells, welcomed by the people who had sorrowed when they saw him leave.[1] The Court, the Bishop, the Magistrates, clergy and people came to visit him as he lay waiting for the final summons. For the first time in forty years he used a bed; he consented to change his hair-shirt for one of rough cloth; and since he absolutely refused to eat flesh-meat, his friends practised a little deception by giving him food which was cooked with fish.[2]

Martin V had asked him what favour he could confer upon him for his services to the Church, and St. Vincent begged for a Plenary Indulgence at the hour of death; he asked for nothing more. This he received, and then he was anointed for the final combat, and received the last Sacraments from Jean Collet, the Vicar of the Cathedral. The people requested to see him that they might receive his blessing once more before he died. Willingly he consented, and from his death-bed blessed those Bretons with a blessing which has never failed. France is apathetic. Her people, many of them, seem to have lost all faith and to have forgotten the glorious traditions of the past : but the Bretons are staunch and loyal still to Jesus Christ and His Church, and Brittany is in truth an oasis in a desert of indifference and unbelief. Shall we not say that

[1] Office of St. Vincent Ferrer for the Diocese of Vannes, *apud* Fages, " Histoire," p. 269.

[2] Evidence of Witnesses, *apud* " Année Dominicaine," p. 229.

St. Vincent Ferrer has been true to the promise
made by him 400 years ago when he told the
Breton people: "I shall be your advocate before
the Throne of God. I shall never fail to im-
plore mercy for you, and I promise that you shall
obtain that mercy if you are faithful to the truth
which I have taught"?[1] The prayers and pleading of God's Saints are stronger than human might
or hellish power.

On the ninth day of his illness, feeling his end
approaching, he had the Passion of Our Lord read
to him, then the Penitential Psalms, after which
he began to recite the Psalter. The Saint and
Wonder-Worker, the Angel of the Judgment, the
mighty preacher of penance who had spent himself
in labouring for the salvation of souls, was soon to
appear before the Judgment Seat himself, and "he
feared with a great fear". As the Psalmist's words
were uttered, and he realized the ineffable sanctity
and inexorable justice of God to Whom he was to
"render an account of his stewardship," beads of
perspiration stood on his forehead, and his voice
shook. It was only for a moment, however, and
peace reigned in his heart, which had never
harboured a treasonable thought. When the Litany
of the Saints had been recited, he who was so soon
to swell the ranks of the heroes of Jesus Christ,
joined his hands and fixed his closing eyes on the
Crucifix which, as he once confessed, was the source

[1] " Histoire," p. 270.

whence all his inspiration came. His face was lit up with sudden rapture. His eyes closed. And the earthly journey of Vincent Ferrer was finished at last. It was the evening of the Wednesday in Passion-Week, 5 April, 1419, and he was in his seventieth year.

Twenty years before he had begun the work of his glorious Apostolate. He had ploughed his furrow, and had sown the seed of truth in the fairest fields of Europe. His day was done. His work was over; and the workman lay dead beside his plough with his face turned towards eternity.[1]

When St. Vincent had expired,—some say before he had breathed his last,—a number of white butterflies flew into the room and fluttered around his head. Those present thought they were angels come to take the Angel of the Judgment home.[2] A piercingly sweet odour exhaled from the dead body, and the Duchess of Brittany, the same Jeanne to whom St. Vincent gave the Rosary beads mentioned in the last chapter, when she had washed the body, perceived the same sweet odour from the water she had used. This water was carefully preserved and many miracles were wrought through its use, while the odour remained until the water itself had evaporated.[3]

[1] Cf. " Histoire," pp. 271-72.

[2] *Ibid.*, " Acta Sanctorum," p. 508.

[3] " Histoire," p. 273; " Acta Sanctorum," p. 509; " Année Dominicaine," pp. 230-31.

The house in which the Saint had died was closed
and barricaded immediately, and by the order of
the Bishop and Chapter a guard was placed inside
and without lest the Dominicans or the Franciscans
should try to remove the body.   Despite these pre-
cautions, however, when Jean Collet came in the
Bishop's name to bear the body of St. Vincent to
the Cathedral, he met with stubborn and almost
angry resistance.   He succeeded nevertheless, and
the body, clothed in the religious habit, was carried
in solemn procession to the Cathedral, where it remained in the choir until Friday, 7 April, exposed
to the veneration of the people who were witnesses
of the suppleness of the limbs, the fresh, clear colour
of the face, and the exquisite perfume which it exhaled.[1]   On Friday, the Saint was buried in the
Cathedral Choir by the Bishop of Vannes, assisted
by the Bishop of Saint-Malo ; and as St. Vincent
had wrought miracles by his touch, nay, by the
touch of his habit during his life, so did his body,
his habit, his very grave seem to be endowed with
miraculous power now.   Two dead persons who
were placed beside the dead Saint were restored
to life, to bear witness to the sanctity of him who
reigned in glory.[2]

Though St. Vincent had said before his death
when those around him asked where he desired to
be buried that he " left everything to the decision

---

[1] " Histoire," p. 274 ; " Acta Sanctorum," p. 509.
[2] *Ibid.*, p. 275 ; cf. " Acta Sanctorum," loc. cit.

of the Bishop of Vannes," it was only natural that
the Order of Preachers, of which he was so illustrious a son, should desire to have the body
amongst his brethren. The Bishop refused to give
up the treasure. The Duke of Brittany also refused; and Nicholas V, by a Bull dated 5 October,
1451, decided that the body of St. Vincent,
"even after his canonization, should remain in the
Cathedral of Vannes ".[1] Still, the Order hoped to
obtain possession of the sacred relics, and on the
day of the Saint's Canonization, the Master-
General, Martial Auribelli, formally requested the
Bishop and Chapter of Vannes to give the body of
St. Vincent into the keeping of the Order. It was
in vain: the request was absolutely refused, and
the refusal was confirmed by another Bull of Pius
II on 9 February, 1460.[2]

Immediately after his death, the process of
St. Vincent's canonization was begun. Miracles
without number were wrought daily at his tomb
and through his intercession; and when a miracle
more extraordinary than others took place the
people of Vannes were notified of it by the ringing
of the city bells, while each Sunday the list of the
miracles which had been wrought during the week
was read out from the pulpit.[3] The request for

[1] " Histoire," p. 278 ; " Notes et Documents," pp. 413-14.

[2] *Ibid.*, pp. 279-80 ; " Notes et Documents," pp. 420-23.

[3] *Ibid.*, p. 313 ; " Année Dominicaine," p. 232.

his canonization was universal. Kings, Bishops, and Universities petitioned the Sovereign Pontiff to enroll this marvellous man amongst the white-robed band of the Saints; while chiefest amongst those who made the request was Frances d'Amboise, already mentioned, who had espoused Pierre, Duke of Brittany. Her efforts were nobly seconded by Pierre himself.[1]

On 18 October, 1451, Nicholas V issued a Bull by which he formally opened the inquiry into the life, heroic sanctity, and miracles of Vincent Ferrer. The Duke of Brittany levied a tax to defray the expenses which the proceedings would necessarily entail.[2] The inquiry was carried on in various places at the same time and was concluded on 7 April, 1454—or according to the Roman Calender, 1455. Eugenius IV, who had succeeded Martin V, was himself succeeded altogether unexpectedly by Alphonsus Borgia who took the name of Calixtus III. Our readers will remember the prophecy which St. Vincent made regarding Alphonsus Borgia many years previously. That prophecy was now to be ful-filled. On 3 June, 1455, Calixtus III declared in full Consistory that on 29 June he would solemnly canonize Vincent Ferrer; and on that day, in the Dominican Church of Santa Maria Sopra

[1] " Histoire," p. 315 *seqq.;* " Acta Sanctorum," p. 521.
[2] The documents are given by Père Fages, " Histoire," pp. 317-21; " Notes et Documents," pp. 381-85.

Minerva in Rome, Calixtus, as Vicar of Jesus
Christ, "pronounced, defined, and decreed that
Vincent Ferrer was a Saint, and that he was to
be venerated as such by the Universal Church".[1]
Calixtus did not publish the Bull of St. Vincent's
Canonization, but his successor, Pius II, published
it on 1 October, 1458.[2] Needless to say there was
great rejoicing at Valencia and in Vannes. At
Vannes on the day of St. Vincent's canonization the
body of the Saint, which was found quite incorrupt,
was once more exposed to the veneration of the
faithful. During the Mass, two dead persons were
covered with the cloak in which St. Vincent had
been buried, and were restored to life in presence
of the vast congregation ; a relative of the Duke of
Brittany was cured of leprosy, and a man who had
been blind from his birth received his sight.[3]

[1] Letter of Calixtus III to the Duke of Brittany,
" Histoire," pp. 331-32. It was this same Pope who ordered
the inquiry for the rehabilitation of Blessed Joan of Arc
(cf. " Jean Bréhal, Grand Inquisiteur de France et La Ré-
habilitation de Jeanne d'Arc," par Les Pères Belou et Balme,
O.P., Paris, 1893, p. 69 *seqq.*).

[2] Cf. " Histoire," pp. 335-43 ; " Acta Sanctorum," p. 523.
The Office of St. Vincent Ferrer was composed by the
Master-General of the Order, Martial Auribelli, who has
signed his name acrostic fashion. The initial letter of each
verse of the Hymn for Vespers, and of the Antiphons for
Matins and Lauds, form the sentence. *Martialis Auribelhi
fecit ;* " Martial Auribelli made me."

[3] Memoir of Falcò and Sala, who were present.
" Histoire," p. 333.

In the following year, on 4 June, 1456, the relics of St. Vincent were enshrined in a new case by the Cardinal Legate, Alain de Coëtivy, in the presence of a large number of Bishops, and a gathering of people which was estimated at 150,000.[1] The Legate forbade any one under the severest penalties to touch the holy relics, but just as the Order of Preachers very naturally desired to obtain possession of them, so also did the city of Valencia. Despite all prohibitions and penalties, the Spaniards determined to take what would not be given to them. The plot was discovered and the body was hidden, remaining in the Sacristy of the Cathedral until 1600, when the countrymen of the Saint again demanded the relics.[2]

In 1637 the relics were removed from the place in which they had been put, were examined by four physicians, and having been duly authenticated, were enclosed in a silver shrine, the gift of the Canons of the Cathedral.[3]

Portions of the relics have been given at various periods to Valencia, Marie Louise of France, the

[1] "Histoire," p. 334; "Acta Sanctorum," p. 523. Razzano, whom the Bollandists follow, gives the date as 5 April, 1456. Père Fages gives the same date in his "Notes et Documents," p. 416.

[2] *Ibid.*, p. 282; cf. "Notes et Documents," p. 435 *seqq.*

[3] *Ibid.*, pp. 284-87; "Acta Sanctorum," pp. 525-27. The relics were again authenticated after examination 1816; cf. "Histoire," pp. 288-90.

Grand-Master of the Knights of Malta and others, but Vannes has been extremely particular in confiding any relics of St. Vincent to any one, and even when Valencia asked for them in 1532, and the request was supported by a Bull of Clement VII, the Chapter at first refused absolutely to accede to it.[1]

We have said that long before his death the Apostle was canonized by the people and called "Saint Vincent". Almost immediately after his death an altar was built near his tomb in the Cathedral at Vannes, and Mass was celebrated regularly in his honour; while Isabella, Duchess of Brittany, founded a Mass to be said in perpetuity at the altar of *Saint* Vincent Ferrer in the Cathedral of Vannes in 1434, that is, eleven years before the Saint was canonized by the Church.[2] When the Saint was formally canonized devotion to him received a new impetus. Benedict XIII (not Peter de Luna but Pietro Orsini, O.P.) indulgenced the devotion of the Seven Fridays preceding the Feast of St. Vincent by a Bull dated 6 February, 1726. These indulgences were confirmed by Clement XII in 1733.[3] The formula of blessing which St. Vincent was accustomed to use for the sick has been adopted by the Dominican Liturgy, and the Saint was chosen as patron by farmers and vine-growers; while he is invoked against thunder-storms and

---

[1] "Histoire," pp. 302-3.　　[2] *Ibid.*, pp. 374-76.
[3] *Ibid.*, p. 379.

earthquakes, and water into which a relic or a
picture of the Saint is placed is blessed by a special
blessing against sickness.   If he is the *"gloria y
delicias del Valentino pueblo"*—the pride and glory
of Valencia, St. Vincent Ferrer is a Saint invoked
throughout the world.   The famous Dominican
Convent of Prato, the home of St. Catherine de'
Ricci, is placed under his protection.   At Florence,
it is the custom to bring little children to the Convent of Santa Maria Novella, there to be blessed
with a relic of St. Vincent; and the sick and ailing
still come to receive the water which has been
blessed in St. Vincent's name.   Italy, indeed, is
remarkable for its devotion to St. Vincent, and in
1836, when even St. Januarius seemed to have forgotten his Neapolitans, during the cholera scourge,
the people turned to St. Vincent Ferrer.   The
cholera ceased.   Naples decreed that the Saint
should be the patron of the city and had a statue of
silver made which is now in the treasury of the Cathedral.[1]   Sicily has named him *" Il Santo delle
Grazie"*—the Saint who confers favours.   Majorca
took him as Patron of the Island.   Confraternities
in his honour exist to the present day in Constanti-
nople, and Russia venerates him as the Apostle of
the East.[2]   St. Leonard of Port Maurice placed
all his work under the protection of our Saint;

[1] "Histoire," pp. 416-23; "Notes et Documents," pp.
496-97.
[2] *Ibid.,* pp. 430-32.

and the Venerable Père Olier, the founder of St. Sulpice, acknowledged that he undertook one of his most important works through the direct intervention of St. Vincent Ferrer. Blessed Nicholas Factor, O.S.F., used to tell all who asked his advice to pray to St. Vincent and that he would assist them ; and the power which the Venerable Father Jerome Lopez, S.J., and Father James Lopez, O.S.A., possessed over sinners was attributed to the devotion these two saintly men had to St. Vincent Ferrer. St. Louis Bertrand's devotion to St. Vincent was extraordinary.   When he was appointed Prior of Valencia he placed the keys of the Convent at the feet of St. Vincent's statue and asked him to govern the Community ; while on one occasion at least he attributed his recovery from a dangerous illness to the intercession of " his father St. Vincent ".[1]   Yes : St. Vincent's name is mighty and his pleading powerful.   The influence of a Saint never grows less, and, as we shall see, that influence in St. Vincent's case was made manifest in life and after his death by the miracles he wrought ; miracles so numerous that they ceased to cause amazement ; yet so astounding as to force us to catch our breath.

[1] Cf. " Life of St. Lewis Bertrand," by Father Wilberforce, O.P., p. 269 *seqq.*, London, 1882.

CHAPTER XI.

THE WONDER-WORKER.

THE supernatural is the atmosphere in which the Saint "lives, moves, and has his being," and in this atmosphere the miraculous is perfectly natural. Modern "science" does not accept the miraculous. It speaks of the miracle as a "contravention of the laws of nature," and in the same breath informs us that we do not know all that nature can do. If this be the case : if we do not yet know all that nature can do, why speak of the *laws of nature ?* The truth is "science" does not want to recognize the supernatural under any circumstances. It strives to deny its existence; and, prejudiced beforehand, it approaches the miraculous in a partial and biased manner, and either rules it out of court or professes to give an explanation of it by purely natural means. This is what has happened in the case of St. Vincent Ferrer. The miracles wrought by him are accounted for by two "scientific" men as the outcome of suggestion, hallucination, telepathy, and second sight.[1] We have no intention of discussing

[1] Cf. Joly, "Psychologie des Saints," VI⁰ Edition, p. 72.

the nature or the possibility of miracles; we only
state now that, while the miraculous is also marvellous, not every marvel is a miracle. The phe-
nomena of Spiritism and Hypnotism are marvellous, many of them: they are not miraculous, for
the miracle is the Divine seal stamped by God
Himself on the work of His servant. The miracle
comes from God, is wrought by God, and leads to
God; and, as we have said before, the miracle is a
sign that he through whose instrumentality it is
wrought is guided by God. There is no natural
explanation of a miracle, because a miracle is wholly
supernatural in our regard; and to attempt to explain by natural means what is absolutely supernatural is to attempt the impossible. Nature has
never raised the dead to life by a word or a touch,
has never given sight instantaneously to a man blind
from his birth, has never restored to life a child
which was killed and hacked in pieces by its mother
in an hour of frenzy. St. Vincent Ferrer was the
man whom God used to do these things; and face
to face with such facts, we are in the presence of
the palpably and manifestly miraculous. Let us
now relate a few of the miracles wrought by our
Saint. We say a few, for the number of authentic
miracles accepted by the Church as proof of the miraculous power of St. Vincent Ferrer, was 873.[1] The
Church is particularly and proverbially strict in

[1] "Histoire," p. 351. The Bollandists give the number
as 860, "Acta Sanctorum," p. 496.

regard to the miracles which are put forward for the canonization of any Saint. They are examined and tested in the severest and most searching manner, and are accepted only when they are clearly miraculous. The Church accepted these 873 miracles of St. Vincent; yet we know that the inquiries held previous to, and in view of, his canonization, were actually closed before a fuller account of the miracles he wrought was obtained. The judges grew tired of the monotonous repetition of the tale of miracles; as the Bishop of Télésia said: "It is quite impossible for me to enumerate all the miracles that I have seen him work, and volumes would not contain them".[1] Some idea of their number may be gathered from the evidence of one witness who followed the Saint for fifteen months, and who testified on oath that, "after Mass and the Sermon, and again after Vespers, the sick were brought to Master Vincent to be healed. Master Vincent laid his hands upon them, blessed them, and the sick were healed and went away rejoicing."[2] We know that the Saint preached every day; and we also know that St. Vincent told the people of Salamanca in 1412, when he announced that he was the Angel of the Apocalypse foretold by St. John, that "until the

---

[1] " Histoire," p. 352. " Considering it would be super-fluous to continue the examination," are the words of the Judges; cf. " Notes et Documents," p. 401.

[2] *Ibid.*, p. 351.

present time God had wrought in His mercy through
him, a miserable sinner, three thousand miracles." [1]
We have already spoken of the miracle which the
Saint wrought to confirm this claim, when he raised
the dead woman to life. St. Antoninus affirms
that twenty-eight persons were raised from death
by St. Vincent, but this does not represent the
total number who were restored to life by the Saint,
great as it is. [2]

In the town of Morella not far distant from
Valencia, the Saint during one of his missions
lodged with a family which was as virtuous as it
was noble. But, alas! there was heartache in the
home, for the wife of his host was attacked
periodically by fits of frenzy. During the Saint's
visit the poor woman was seized with one of these
attacks. She killed her child; and, cutting the
body in pieces, began to prepare it with the other
food for dinner. When her husband returned
from the Sermon, it was only to find that his little
son had been cruelly murdered. He became wild
with grief, and began to blaspheme and to lay the
blame on St. Vincent. The Saint entered the
house shortly afterwards, and on being told what
had occurred, ordered the mangled body to be
brought to him. Then kneeling down he prayed:
" May Jesus Christ the Son of Mary, the Lord and
Saviour of the world, Who drew the soul of this
child from nothingness, restore it once again to its

[1] " Histoire," Vol. I, p. 315. [2] *Ibid.*,Vol. II, p. 344.

body, to the praise and glory of His great majesty". In the presence of the parents and of those neighbours whom the cries of the husband had brought to the house, the members of the child's body were united, one to the other. The child was restored to life and lived for many years.[1] Another miracle exactly similar occurred at Vannes after the Saint's death. This time, however, the father of the child rushed to St. Vincent's tomb and poured forth his request in tears and prayers. When the hour for closing the church came, the poor man was afraid to go home, but when he did it was to find his child alive and well in his cradle, yet with the marks of the knife plainly visible, marks which were never effaced. The child's name was Vincent Pistoia, and he' became a Dominican in later years.[2] The Register of the Dominican Convent at Bologna mentions under the date, 15 April, 1481, that on this day "Brother Vincent of Bologna, who was restored to life through the merits and intercession of St. Vincent Ferrer, received the habit". In 1564, this youth, then an old man of 92, was present at the General Chapter of the Order which was held in Bologna. He died thirteen years later. St. Vincent had evidently restored him to length of years as well as to life.[3]

[1] " Histoire," Vol. II., pp. 53-54 ; " Acta Sanctorum," p. 501.

[2] " Histoire," Vol. II., pp. 369-70.

[3] *Ibid.*, p. 371 ; cf. " Notes et Documents," p. 376.

Another class of miracles wrought by St. Vincent during his life and after his death, was the expulsion of devils from the persons possessed or obsessed by them. We are quite aware that certain writers grow sarcastic over the accounts given in Holy Scripture and the lives of the Saints of diabolical possession, and profess to explain all such occurrences by nervous disorders or epilepsy. It may come as a surprise, however, to hear so eminent an authority as Mr. Godfrey Raupert state emphatically that even at the present day cases of diabolical possession are not so rare as is commonly supposed.[1] The Bollandists state that seventy possessed persons were freed by St. Vincent Ferrer;[2] and one of those who gave evidence during the process of inquiry asserts that, "when the possessed persons were brought into the Saint's presence, the demon fled before the usual Exorcism prescribed by the Church was recited."[3] What occurred during St. Vincent's lifetime occurred frequently after his death, and it was the custom to bring the unhappy persons so afflicted to the tomb of the Saint. There they were set free through the intercession of him who had been the scourge of Satan and his satellites during his life.[4] The Bre-

[1] Cf. "Dangers of Spiritualism," Appendix, London, 1906; and the article "Spiritistic Perils," by the same author in the "Austral Light," September, 1906.

[2] "Acta Sanctorum," p. 503.   [3] "Histoire," Vol. II, p. 353.

[4] Cf. "Histoire," *ibid.*, pp. 354-55; "Acta Sanctorum," p. 509.

ton fishermen invoked our Saint when they were in
danger of shipwreck, and there are many instances
on record where St. Vincent came to their assistance when no human power could have saved
them.[1]   In fact there was hardly a disease by which
humanity could be afflicted that was not cured by
the Saint in his lifetime, or through his intercession
after his death.   The almost dry pages of the
" Acta Sanctorum," so precise, so critical, are eloquent in their account of the miracles wrought by
this wonderful man.   A woman of Toulouse, who
had for many years been a victim to excruciating
pains in her head was cured instantaneously by
placing the Saint's hat on her head.   Another
woman, the mother of Theobald Lasset, had her
sight restored immediately on making a vow to
visit the Saint's tomb.   Numerous cases of persons
dying of the plague and restored to health by calling on St. Vincent, are recorded; while several
cures from the loathsome disease of leprosy are
well authenticated.   The blind and lame, the
deaf and dumb, turned to this Saint in their ex-
tremity, confident that he who had never refused
to exercise the power God had given him in life,
would not refuse to hearken to their prayers now
that he reigned in glory.   It would be utterly impossible to narrate the cures effected by the Saint.
What we have said regarding the number of miracles

[1] Cf. Histoire," Vol. II, pp. 358-61; "Acta Sanctorum,"
pp. 513, 515.

accepted by the Church is sufficient to show that St. Vincent Ferrer deserved the title of Wonder-Worker. Four hundred sick persons were cured by merely resting on the couch on which the Saint had lain,[1] while the *ex-voto* offerings in thanksgiving for the cures effected through his intercession is beyond count. The Venerable Louis of Grenada used to say that St. Vincent worked miracles as naturally as we should move our hands; and that if we would number them we must also count the stars of heaven. He is our authority for the statement that no inquiry was held in Spain itself into the miraculous powers of the Saint. One incident must be related before we conclude this chapter, the astounding occurrence which took place at Zamora in 1412.

One day that the Saint was preaching in this town, two persons were led to execution. The penalty was death by burning. The Saint requested the officers of justice to bring the two condemned before him. This was done, and the criminals were placed on the pulpit-steps, hidden from the eyes of the people. St. Vincent began to speak of the punishment which sin met with in the other life and then, in vivid terms, depicted the sin of which the two condemned had been guilty and the penalty it deserved. His sermon lasted three hours, but when the authorities went to remove the condemned it was discovered that remorse had

[1] " Histoire," p. 374.

done its work in a striking and effective manner, for they were burnt by some mysterious fire to the very bones.[1]   The bodies of the criminals were buried near the pulpit from which the Saint had preached. The learned and saintly Cornelius a Lapide, S.J., in his "Commentary on Jeremias," mentions this incident, affirming that "the exhortations of St. Vincent were productive of such grief in the hearts of the two criminals as to cause their death as if by fire.   Repentance and love were their executioners; rather should we say repentance and love gave them new life." [2]

It was by his miracles that St. Vincent confirmed the truths which he preached; it was these same miracles which struck deep and strong at hearts hardened in sin, and softened them.   The conversions he effected were standing miracles, and to change a sinful heart is a greater miracle than to cure the leper, or give sight to the blind, or speech to the dumb, for such a conversion demands a change of will, and a will which has been enervated by pleasure or made obstinate by pride is difficult to change.   We have seen how the Saint succeeded, how sinners cried for mercy, and joined the ranks of his penitents.   We have seen that, according to the Jews, 200,000 of their number were received into the Church in conse-

---

[1] "Histoire," Vol. I, p. 304; "Acta Sanctorum," p. 511.
[2] *Ibid.* pp. 305-6; "Notes et Documents," pp. 204-5.

quence of the preaching of this man. A Saint's influence never dies ; and St. Vincent Ferrer, the Wonder-Worker and Angel of the Judgment, is as powerful now before God as in the days of his mortal life. This thought is one to encourage us, and to urge us to have confidence in, and recourse to him "that he may be propitious to us in the evening of life, and bring us safely to Jesus Christ ".

CHAPTER XII.

THE SAINT AND HIS TEACHING.

WE only speak absolute truth when we say that St. Vincent Ferrer would never have been the marvellous preacher and Saint that he was if he had not been a Dominican. Each Order has its peculiar spirit, an atmosphere special to itself. St. Vincent was a member of the Order of Preachers ; and while he is one of the brightest examples of the spirit and training of the Order, he was fashioned in the mould which is peculiar to that Order and became what he was by being a Dominican. He was first and foremost a preacher, but he was a Dominican preacher, trained according to the Dominican ideal. That ideal is shown forth on the first pages of the Dominican Constitutions : *Contemplare, et aliis contemplata tradere :* to contemplate, and then to give the fruits of his contemplation to others. Every Saint is a man of prayer ; but each Saint prays in his own way. St. Vincent was a man of prayer after the Dominican standard which was based upon the ancient monastic ideal, and in which the Choral Office and

Liturgy are provided for in fulness and solemnity. Hence we have seen that the Saint sang Mass every morning and had a body of priests to sing the Proper of the Mass. He was only carrying out on his missionary journeys the same solemn ceremonial in which he had been trained at Valencia. He rose at two o'clock to recite the Divine Office chorally. After Matins it was his custom to recite the Psalter privately, then to read the Sacred Scriptures which he seemed to know by heart, or to give himself up to close communion with God by contemplation. Like St. Dominic he scourged himself to blood night after night in reparation for his own sins and those of the world. He confessed his sins—how few, and in our eyes how trivial must they not have been,—every morning before Mass, which he sang at six in summer and at seven during the winter months. After Mass he preached, and we learn that the sermon usually lasted three hours. Then came the blessing of the sick who came from all parts, for the blessing of " Master Vincent " carried bodily healing with it. At 1 o'clock he broke his fast. Marshal Boucicaut informs us that the Saint "took but one dish, the first that was offered to him ; he refused all sauces and savouries ; and the little wine that he drank was scarcely worthy of the name so well diluted was it with water." [1]

[1] " Livre des faicts du Maréchal Boucicaut," quoted in " Histoire," Vol. I, p. 160.

Never under any circumstance did he eat flesh meat, and for forty years he observed a continual fast every day, except Sundays, making the fast stricter on Wednesdays and Fridays, eating only the one meal each day, and that a very meagre affair. After his repast he retired, not to take the "siesta" which is a necessity in southern countries, but to recite the remainder of his Office, then to catechize the children and the ignorant, to visit the sick-poor, the needy, and afflicted, to listen to the tales of sin and sorrow that were poured into his ears, and to lecture to any nuns who might have Convents in the district.

At eight o'clock he prepared his discourse for the following day, and at nine he retired to rest, if rest it could be called, since he slept on the floor with a stone, or a block of wood, for a pillow. This was his daily life during the twenty years of his apostolate.[1]

Some, perhaps, may think that after all there was nothing so very extraordinary in such a life. But we would first of all repeat the commonplace by reminding our readers that true holiness of life does not consist in doing the extraordinary, but in doing the ordinary duties of life extraordinarily well. Secondly, we would ask those who might make objection to bear in mind the circumstances of the times in which St. Vincent lived. There were no railways in those days, no easy journeys, and St.

[1] Cf. " Histoire," pp. 445-66; " Acta Sanctorum," p. 491.

Vincent travelled through Spain, France, and the north of Italy on foot—for it was only in the last years of his life, when an ulcer in his leg made walking impossible, that he consented to ride on an ass. He was exposed to the inclemency of all weathers; to the fierce, burning heats of the south, and to the keen, biting winds of the north. He travelled over rough roads where roads existed, but more frequently he was compelled to cross almost impassable mountain ranges, swollen rivers, and rocky defiles in his zeal for the salvation of souls. He had to put up with all the inconveniences such a method of travelling entailed, and the fact that he was a Saint did not make him feel those inconveniences the less. Though he practised austerities, so that his life was one continual fast, and though he did these things for Christ's sake, he felt the pangs of hunger, and the shrinkings of his natural feelings from pain, none the less keenly. When we remember these things, and remember too the weariness, and exhaustion, and decrease of energy which preaching entails, specially when the preacher was a Vincent Ferrer; when we remember that day after day he lived the self-same life, without any change or break, that he lived as if he had been within the cloister, we come to realize that St. Vincent was more than an ordinary man, and that his life was in the highest degree an extraordinary life.

Added to the labours of an Apostle were the anxieties of a counsellor of Kings who consulted

him on affairs of State; of Magistrates who pleaded
with him to come and put an end to the strife which
was the ruin of many a city in Europe; of theologians who laid their doubts and difficulties before
him; and of sinners who came to him as others
came to the Feet of Jesus Christ to lay the burden
of their sin and shame upon the shoulders of one
who was only too willing to bear it. Was it an
easy thing to be the confidant of a Pope who was
obstinate? Was it easy to plead with one whom he
recognized as the Vicar of Christ, and to urge him
to lay aside his tiara when the interests of the
Church demanded it? And was it without a pang
that our Saint gave that decision for which a
Council of the Church waited in breathless expecta-
tion since he alone could bring about peace, when
the giving of it meant the breaking of a friendship
which had lasted many years? Saints are human;
and it is hard for a Saint, as it is for a sinner, to
break with friends. And did not the care of his
band of Penitents cause him many an anxious
moment, lest any scandal might arise, or the enemy
of souls find an entrance into those hearts which
once had harboured him and which were always in
danger of harbouring him again? It was no wonder
that his beauty seemed to fade, and that he grew
feeble, and weary, and longed like another Apostle
"to be dissolved and to be with Christ".

And this man who thrilled and captivated the
hearts of Europe by his burning words; whose

arguments proved irresistible to Jew and Saracen; whose word called back the dead to life; whose touch gave sight and healing; nay, whose very habit was endowed with miraculous power, was only a poor, humble Friar-Preacher, worn and weak from long journeys, and much preaching, and vigils and fasts. But he was a living image of the Crucified, and therein was the secret of his success. Kind, gentle, patient, and forbearing, he was never known to murmur though he had frequent cause to do so. Poorest of the poor he was, and the first pages of his "Treatise on the Spiritual Life" are a reflex of his own poverty of Spirit. There he tells us to be content with what is strictly necessary, and by the strictly necessary St. Vincent means : "A little food, coarse clothing, and a pair of shoes"! Speaking of purity of heart in the same treatise, St. Vincent says that he does not speak of that "purity which implies the exclusion of all sinful thoughts, but of that chastity and purity of heart which makes us shun as far as possible all useless thoughts, in order that we may cling to God alone." [1] We know that the Saint practised what he preached. His purity of heart was remarkable even in a Saint, and was made manifest to others by the exquisite perfume which exhaled from his body, the sweet aroma of virginal chastity. And the first means given by the Saint to preserve this purity, namely obedience, was so faithfully observed by him, that

[1] "Traité de la Vie Spirituelle," ed. Rousset, p. 25.

as one witness acknowledged, "no novice sheltered within the hallowed walls of the novitiate was ever more humbly submissive to the commands of his superiors ". No need to say that he was humble, his whole demeanour was eloquent testimony of the low esteem in which he held himself; and thus he could say that "though pride came and went it never stayed ". If he could startle sinners by the thunders of his eloquence when he preached on the Last Judgment, he could move even the hardest to tears when he preached on the Passion of Our Lord, or devotion to the Mother of God. Never was he so winning in his simple pathos as when he spoke of the sufferings of Jesus Christ; never did his voice ring with such genuine emotion as when he preached on the glories of Mary Immaculate. We say "Mary Immaculate " advisedly, for St. Vincent Ferrer taught and preached the doctrine of the Immaculate Conception of Our Blessed Lady.[1] It was St. Vincent, as tradition has it, who introduced the custom of reciting the *Ave Maria* before the Sermon. In one of his discourses during Holy Week he said : "We shall not address Our Lady to-day in the usual manner, for could she not ask us, if we did so : How can you say *Hail !* to me who am sad and sorrow-stricken ? How can you say :

---

[1] "Sermons," II, On the Nativity; On the Immaculate Conception. Cf. Lepicier, O.S.M., " Tractatus de Beatissima Virgine Maria," p. 119; Hugon, O.P., "La Mère de Grâce," p. 25, and note.

The Lord is with thee, when they have taken away my Son and have nailed Him to a Cross? And how can you call me *Blessed* since every voice is lifted up against me?" The simple words were uttered in so gentle and sorrowful a tone that all who heard them began to weep bitterly, and to cry for pardon and mercy.[1]

When we come to think of the marvellous effects of St. Vincent's preaching we are not surprised to find that all classes, priests and learned theologians as well as unlettered people, were loud in their praise of the Apostle. Like his Divine Master who " began to do and to teach," our Saint gave force to his words by the example of his life. He was simple yet profound in his discourses, eminently practical, and he drove his lessons home by means of homely examples. This was his advice to other preachers too ; " Be simple," he tells us; "be practical; eschew all general statements and come to particular things, illustrating your teaching by examples. Let not your language be harsh ; never show anger, but act as a tender father would act towards his children who are sick ; act as a mother who caresses her children and encourages them, and who rejoices at the progress they have made." [2] It was by his gentleness that St. Vincent reclaimed the sinners who "like sheep had gone astray".

[1] " Histoire," p. 452.
[2] " Traité de la Vie Spirituelle," *ut supra,* pp. 137-38.

Severe in his denunciations of sin, he was ever tender and compassionate towards the sinner ; and in this as in all else he was only following in the footsteps of his Father St. Dominic.   He had set himself to imitate St. Dominic, when he received the religious habit in Valencia ; and the life of the Founder of the Friars-Preachers became his constant study.   That life told him that St. Dominic was accustomed to spend almost the whole night in prayer, and when sleep did overcome him that he slept with his head resting on the altar step, or leaning against the wall.   He read that his Father used to scourge himself thrice each night with an iron chain ; that he wept often, particularly during Holy Mass, that his greatest joy was to be despised ; that sin and suffering were a continual source of anguish to him ; and that he preserved his virginal purity in all its freshness until his death.   He learned that his fast was unbroken, and that never, even during sickness, would he eat flesh meat ; that nó deadly sin ever sullied his soul ; that his speech was either with God or of God ; that so great was his zeal for souls that he yearned to die a martyr's death.   Wonder-Worker during his life, innumerable miracles were wrought at his tomb after his death, and the Church in her Offices had styled him a man of Apostolic spirit, a staunch defender of the faith, a sublime herald of the Gospel, a light of the world, a dazzling reflection

of Jesus Christ, a Rose of patience, another pre-
cursor, and a master in the science of souls.
St. Vincent read these things and they urged
him to imitation.   We read them, and we may
apply the description of the Father to one of his
greatest sons.   The disciple was worthy of the
master; worthy, too, to wear the crown wherewith
he has been crowned by God; and therefore do
we pray to him that he may plead for us.   May St.
Vincent be our advocate.   May he plead for the
Church he served so loyally and well, that the days
of her sorrows may be shortened, and that peace
may be given her once again.

> " *Adsit nobis propitius in hujus Vitæ Vespere,*
> *Ad Christum nos Vincentius, tuto ferens itinere.*"
> Be gracious, Vincent, unto us
>   In this life's eventide !
> Guide thou our long lone journeying
>   Unto Christ's side.

BIBLIOGRAPHY.

The following books with a few others mentioned in the text have been consulted in the preparation of this sketch.

"Histoire de Saint Vincent Ferrier," 2 vols., par Le Père Fages, O.P., Nouvelle Edition. Paris, Louvain, 1901.

"Notes et Documents de l'Histoire de Saint Vincent Ferrier," par Le Père Fages, O.P. Paris, Louvain, 1905.

"Acta Sanctorum." Aprilis. Tom. I., 476-527. Ed. Palme. Romæ, Parisiis, MDCCCLXV. Including lives by (a) Peter Rouzanus, 1455; (b) Francis Castiglione, 1470; (c) Bernard Guyard, 1634.

"Année Dominicaine." Nouvelle Edition, Jevain. Avril. Lyon, 1889.

"Vie de St. Vincent Ferrier," par L'Abbé Bayle. Paris, 1855.

"Three Catholic Reformers," by Mary H. Allies. London, 1878.

"Histoire des Maîtres Generaux de l'Ordre des Frères Prêcheurs," par Le Père Mortier, O.P. Tom. IV. Paris, 1909.

" History of the Popes," by Dr. Ludwig Pastor. English Translation, Third Edition. London, 1906.

" Psychologie des Saints," par Henri Joly. Sixième Edition, Paris, 1900.

"Les Dons du Saint-Esprit dans les Saints Dominicains," par Le Père Gardeil, O.P. Paris, 1903.

" Traité de la Vie Spirituelle de Saint Vincent Ferrier." Edition Rousset, O.P. Paris, 1893.

"Instructio Vitæ Spiritualis." Mechilinæ, 1886.

" Summa Theologica Sancti Thomæ Aquinatis," II^{a} II^{æ}.

" Quæstiones Disputatæ, Sancti Thomæ Aquinatis. De Veritate."

"Traité de la Vie Interieure." 2 vols., par Le Père Meynard, O.P. Paris, 1899.